Economics, Ethics and the Environment

Cavendish
Publishing
Limited

London • Sydney

Economics, Ethics and the Environment

Papers from the UKELA Cardiff Conference, June 2001

Edited by
Julian Boswall
Planning and Environment Group, Morgan Cole

Robert Lee
Professor of Law, Cardiff Law School

Cavendish
Publishing
Limited

London • Sydney

First published in Great Britain 2002 by Cavendish Publishing Limited,
The Glass House, Wharton Street, London WC1X 9PX, United Kingdom
Telephone: +44 (0)20 7278 8000   Facsimile: +44 (0)20 7278 8080
Email: info@cavendishpublishing.com
Website: www.cavendishpublishing.com

British Library Cataloguing in Publication Data

Boswall, Julian
Economics, ethics and the environment
1 Environmental law – England 2 Environmental law – Wales
3 Environmental ethics 4 Environmental law, International
I Title II Lee, Robert G ·

ISBN 1 85941 725 6

Printed and bound in Great Britain

CONTRIBUTORS

Hilary Neal is currently acting head of the European Wildlife Division of the Department of Environment, Transport and the Regions (DETR). The Division's work spans policy on all aspects of wildlife conservation in England, including species and habitat protection and biodiversity. In consultation with the devolved administrations, it also formulates and presents the UK position and response to European nature conservation policies within the relevant multilateral conventions, agreements and treaties. Hilary was formerly head of the Division's Biodiversity Policy Unit. The Unit provides the secretariat for the UK Biodiversity Group which oversees the implementation of the UK Biodiversity Action Plan as part of national implementation of the Convention on Biological Diversity. It also provides secretariat services for the England Biodiversity Group and promotes and co-ordinates the implementation of government policy on the conservation of biodiversity. The Biodiversity Policy Unit also oversees the UK response to the Bern Convention on the Conservation of European Wildlife and Natural Habitats and the Pan-European Biological and Landscape Diversity Strategy.

Hilary Neal took up this post in early September 1999. For eight years previously she had responsibility within the European Wildlife Division for the implementation of the Natura 2000 aspects of the EC Habitats and Birds Directives. She was part of the UK Government team which participated in negotiations leading to adoption of the European Union Habitats Directive and the preparation of the Conservation (Natural Habitats etc) Regulations 1994.

Julian Boswall is the head of the Planning and Environment Group at Morgan Cole. He is based in Cardiff, but works across the firm's five offices from London to Swansea. He has specialised in environmental and planning law throughout his legal career, beginning at Cameron Markby Hewitt, via Clifford Chance and joining Morgan Cole in 1998. Specialist areas in which he works include waste management, contaminated land, power projects and defending environmental prosecutions. In terms of the session which he chaired at the Conference, he has advised his fair share of US companies operating in or investing in the UK, and is increasingly involved with environmental insurance on corporate and property transactions. He is a council member of UKELA.

Michael Quint has recently joined PB Environment in London as a technical director. He has more than 12 years' experience of assessing environmental risks and liabilities and has helped to develop government guidance in these areas. Mike was educated at Oxford University and has spent five years working as an environmental consultant in the USA. Before joining PB Environment he worked for Dames and Moore, during which time he set up and managed a European risk assessment group. In this capacity, he directed numerous projects around Europe and had overall responsibility for environmental and reputational risk assessment. Mike's skills range from strategy formulation to technical analysis, and from issues, identification to reputation management. He has provided expert evidence on environmental matters to several public inquiries, a civil court, the Royal Commission on Environmental Pollution and a Parliamentary select committee. He recently edited *Environmental Impact of Chemicals: Assessment and Control* (1996, Cambridge: The Royal Society of Chemistry) and was a contributing author to Blackwells' *Handbook of Environmental Risk Assessment and Management* (1997, Oxford: Blackwell Science). He is currently on the editorial board of *Land Contamination and Reclamation* (1998, Oxford: Blackwell Science).

Allan Rickmann has more than 25 years' experience in the fields of environmental protection and occupational health and safety and five years' experience in environmental insurance broking. He is currently director of Safety for Sypol Ltd. He is a physicist with postgraduate qualifications in occupational hygiene. His background includes being a research scientist, developing commercial laboratory services from start-up, and being managing director of a leading health, safety and environmental consultancy. He has sat on the Council of the Institute of Environmental Management and Assessment and on the Confederation of British Industry Environmental Affairs Committee.

Anthony Hobley is a senior solicitor with Baker and McKenzie, London. He holds a first class honours degree in chemistry with physics and is a graduate of the Royal Society of Chemistry. He has been a member of UKELA since 1989. He qualified as a solicitor in 1994, since when he has specialised in environment law. He is secretary to the UK Environmental Law Group, Working Group on Climate Change, chairs the Emissions Trading Group Legal Liaison Sub-group on Compliance and Governance and has advised both a major trade association and industry clients on Climate Change Levy Agreements. He advises UK, overseas and multinational clients, including government departments, on all aspects of environment law, both contentious and non-contentious. He has been recommended in the environment law section of the *Chambers Guide to the Legal Profession* (2001, London: Chambers & Partners) for the last two years.

Mike Radford is based in the School of Law at the University of Aberdeen. Primarily a public lawyer, he developed an interest in animal welfare law some 10 years ago, and he now regards this as his principal area of research. Among his current responsibilities he is a member of the Council of the Universities Federation for Animal Welfare (UFAW), a committee member of the Animal Welfare Science, Ethics and Law Veterinary Association (AWSELVA) and a member of the Companion Animal Welfare Council (CAWC). He is also an academic adviser to, and external examiner for, the Royal College of Veterinary Surgeons. Mike is the author of *Animal Welfare Law in Britain* (2001, Oxford: OUP). He is currently updating the 'animals' volume of *Halsbury's Laws of England* (London: Butterworths) and undertaking research, funded by the Royal Society for the Prevention of Cruelty to Animals, into the licensing of animal establishments by local authorities.

Robert Lee is a Professor of Law at, and the former head of, Cardiff Law School where he now acts as Chair of the Cardiff Foundation of Environmental Research. Along with colleagues from the Business and Planning Schools at Cardiff, he has recently been awarded a research grant to found the first Economic and Social Research Council Centre in Wales which will address the theme of business relationships accountability, sustainability and society. Bob has wide practice experience in environmental law and his academic interests tend to concern issues at the interface of health and environment, including regulation of biomedicine and problems of toxic torts. He is author of a book on the regulation of *Human Fertilisation and Embryology* (2001, Oxford: OUP) was published by OUP in 2001. Bob is editor of *Environmental Law Monthly* and environmental editor of the *Journal of Business Law*. He is a member of the Training Committee of the Law Society of England and Wales and of the Lord Chancellor's Standing Committee on Legal Education.

Peter Kellett is a solicitor. He has worked for the Environment Agency for almost four years. He spent his first two years with the Agency working in the its Thames Region office, advising upon operational decisions. Since then, Peter has worked upon national issues for the Agency's head office legal services directorate team, based in Bristol. Prior to joining the Agency, Peter worked in a commercial law firm in a specialist environmental services unit. Peter's current responsibilities include advising upon day to day issues of consistency for Integrated Pollution Prevention and Control (IPPC) nationally, training Agency staff upon the IPPC regime, advising upon radioactive substances legislation and assisting with national litigation. Peter has a masters degree in environmental law and is the advisory editor of the recent *Encyclopaedia of Forms and Precedents* (London: Butterworths) volume on environment.

Stephen Tromans is a barrister. He has been interested in environmental law since the early 1980s, when he was lecturing at Cambridge. He was one of the original founders of UKELA. He practised environmental law as a solicitor for 12 years, most of them running the environmental department at Simmons and Simmons. He then got fed up with being an administrator rather than a lawyer and, in 1999, switched over to the Bar, where he is now a member of 39 Essex Street (Chambers of Nigel Pleming QC). He has written the odd environmental tome, and has acted from time to time as a specialist legal adviser to Committees in both Houses of Parliament. He is a council member of English Nature (since 1996) and is a trustee of Forum for the Future.

FOREWORD

The UK Environmental Law Association (UKELA)[1] Annual Conference can claim to be the leading law conference in the UK for academics, practitioners and students both of law and of a much wider range of disciplines relating to the environment. Indeed, the breadth of interest is reflected in the conference theme of economics, ethics and the environment, and an attendance of some 200 delegates at the Cardiff Conference in June 2001 demonstrated the interest in a programme that looked at both wider ranging environmental questions alongside matters of day to day environmental regulation. The variety of the subject matter is represented in the papers published here.

The conference moved from a traditional slot around Easter to a date at the end of June. The delightful June weather allowed delegates to take full advantage of choice tours around Cardiff Bay, the Museum of Welsh Life, the Millennium Stadium (which was hosting the Wales Motor Show) and, for the truly dedicated, Europe's largest sewage works. Barbara Young opened the conference on the Friday evening by setting out the agenda of the Environment Agency as it related to the conference themes. Saturday evening was spent at the gala dinner in the impressive setting of the National Museum of Wales, to which we were welcomed by the Counsel General of the Welsh Assembly, Winston Roddick QC.

There are many acknowledgments due in this Foreword to those who made the conference a success, beginning with everyone who spoke or chaired the lively conference sessions on the following topics:

- International Law and Enforcement.
- Risk and Insurance.
- Carbon Law.
- Boundaries of Environmental Law and Ethical Issues.
- Waste Management and Regulation.

This year saw larger conference sponsorship than ever before, thanks mainly to the unstinting efforts of Julian Boswall. Agreement to sponsor the conference as a whole by Homecheck and by ERM made an enormous difference to the conference organisers in planning and budgeting for the event. Other sponsors of key parts of the conference included Certa, the IT Group, Environ, Butterworths, Gibb and HSBC. In addition, a number of organisations chose to exhibit either at the conference itself or through the delegate pack. This included the present publishers of this text, Cavendish Publishing – for whose further assistance in bringing the papers to print we are enormously grateful – along with Blackstone, Churngold, Landmark, Mowlem, SRK and the Welsh Development Agency.

---

1   For details of UKELA members, contact: join@ukela.org.

On behalf of the membership of UKELA, I should like to thank also Cardiff Law School and Morgan Cole. A host of people worked on their behalf or were dragooned by them to help with the conference. In addition to the splendid keynote contributions mentioned above by Barbara Young and Winston Roddick, the conference organisers have asked me to thank, especially, the Cardiff University Conference Unit and in particular Su Hayward-Lewis and Samantha Hicks; also Hyder, Cardiff Harbour Authority, David Crompton OBE, Cliff Penny, Linda Brooks, Rhiannon Evans, Russell Price, Ashima Arora, Clare Pike, Tony Caffel, Anthony Hobley, William Upton, Valerie Fogleman and the UKELA Council.

Finally, the UKELA Council would like to thank the conference organisers, Julian Boswall and Robert Lee. The publication of these papers completes their work on the Cardiff Conference and I look forward to seeing many friends and colleagues in UKELA at the conference in Sheffield on 28–30 June 2002.

Pamela Castle
Chair of UKELA
March 2002

CONTENTS

CHAPTER 1

ECONOMICS, ETHICS AND THE ENVIRONMENT

Julian Boswall[1] and Robert Lee[2]

Welfare economics has at its heart a concept that an individual actor will behave rationally so as to maximise utility. Indeed, utility might be seen as the product of the expression of those individual preferences. In this framework, the consumer is sovereign and best placed to determine what is in his or her own welfare. We might expect, logically, that people are behaving so as to make themselves better off. Economists then argue that a working and efficient market should emerge out of this individualism, constructed from the sum of its parts. However, this hypothesis rests on a number of assumptions, including that these actors respond competitively to maximise their utility on the basis of full information. Even if they do so, there may be other external costs or benefits (externalities) that may disrupt the allocative efficiency hoped for by the economists. These externalities are of great interest to those concerned with environmental regulation because the environment itself may provide benefits or create costs not fully accounted for by those making use of it. But, before exploring externalities, a word about ethics ...

The idea of individuals competing to advance their own wealth is not necessarily attractive on the face of it. However, the economist might reply that consumer sovereignty allows a range of choices to the individual and it is open to that person to express a true preference rather than one that seems to be the manifestly advantageous choice. Another way of putting this is that utility might be derived from the freedom to act in a manner which would not seem, on the face of it, to be to the selfish advantage of the individual. Thus, the utility derived by the individual consists not only of the outcome of market choice, but also of the process by which that outcome was achieved. This is important to remember when dealing with environmental regulation, especially where we may hope that consumers may act in a manner which might incur costs (such as the opportunity cost attaching to a slower and less flexible journey by public transport). We can influence choice by so called market instruments (changing the relative costs of pursuing certain options) but, ultimately, it assists greatly to have people buy into the notion of protecting the environment.

---

1   Partner, Morgan Cole, Cardiff.
2   Professor of Law and co-director of the Economic and Social Research Council Research Centre on Business Relationships, Accountability, Sustainability and Society, Cardiff University.

The problem which may arise, however, is whether the results of such individually rational behaviour will prove collectively desirable. In broad terms, is economic welfare advanced and allocative efficiency reached? Judging allocative efficiency is by no means easy, but economists frequently invoke notions of Pareto optimality.[3] The allocation is deemed to be efficient where the welfare of at least one individual is advanced without retarding the welfare of any other person. However, this is not the only possible measure. Concern about the practicality of achieving a position in which the allocation of resources is altered to the detriment of no one has helped promote the Kalder-Hicks[4] criterion. This examines the advancement of welfare by asking the question whether the winners are in a position to compensate those losing and still make an overall gain.

As with all issues in welfare economics, this can be a useful measure at the policy level when seeking to assess the impact of altering resource allocations, but one should be wary of employing the equation normatively. The mere fact that the winners are in a position to compensate effectively the losers, does not mean that they are ever likely to do so. Indeed, the formula may offend notions of distributive justice by, in effect, permitting one set of persons to impose losses on others. Even in the Pareto formulation, the measure of social desirability of change is unashamedly utilitarian. However, many economists would assert the inherent justice of the market in seeking always to extend choice and support the autonomous decisions of individuals. On the other hand, the Pareto optimal position may be said to legitimate the entire enterprise of utility maximisation. Other ethical viewpoints are inevitably subjugated. While economists claim that issues of value can be incorporated into economic models, so that much work has sought to place a value upon the environment itself, the type of ethical position propounded by Mike Radford in his essay on animal protection is not easy to accommodate within an economic framework. This is because utilitarian arguments are implicitly anthropocentric.

Regulation is generally called for in situations of market failure and in order to intervene to influence the context in which individual choices are exercised in order to correct the failure. Thus, there are inextricable links between these issues of economics ethics and (environmental) regulation. One depiction of neo-classical economics might be that individual rationality, pursued all around us, produces an institutional framework from bottom up. However, where this fails, then the government intervenes out of necessity,

---

3   Pareto, V, *Manual of Political Economy*, Schwier, AS (trans), in Schwier, AS and Page, AN (eds), 1971, New York: AM Kelley.

4   See Kaldor, N, 'Welfare propositions in economics and inter-personal comparisons of utility' (1939) 49 Economic Journal 549; Hicks, J, 'The foundations of welfare economics' (1939) 49 Economic Journal 696; and Hicks, J, 'The valuation of social income' (1940) 7 Economica 105.

from top down, in order to assert corrective control in the wider public interest. In one respect, this places the government as an ethical actor, but actually only in the narrow utilitarian terms of the welfare economic framework. Many would hope for a more pluralist approach in which other ethical viewpoints are considered and not rendered redundant, or suppressed by the narrow workings of rationality. Holding middle ground between competing ethical viewpoints is a considerable task, but it depicts government not as a top down enterprise, but as a democratic endeavour to promote social agreement through ethical debate.

Quite where one sits in relation to these issues will determine absolutely one's view of environmental regulation, and there are enormous tensions between the two positions. On the one hand, adherence to the market philosophy with its more disciplined approach to the correction of market failure to restore the power of the invisible hand offers a structured and coherent approach to problems of environmental regulation. A more pluralist approach has the tendency for a free for all in which sight of the goal of environmental regulation may be lost and regulatory mechanisms may be ill-defined. Indeed, this division is likely to influence the legal instruments employed in the regulatory task. Proponents of a market based approach will look naturally towards private law models which offer implicit support for the individual autonomy necessary to drive rational choice. Those disposed to wider State intervention will generally propose public law models and have generally pursued the use of administrative law models to determine the relative allocation of rights to access resources, backed by criminal sanctions to remedy breaches of the conditions upon which that allocation has been made. Proponents of this public law framework would argue that it promotes a more inclusive approach to achieving the common good.

It is idle to pretend that private law rights will solve all problems relating to the use of environmental resources. This is because the problems of externalities in relation to the environment will prove so pervasive that private law mechanisms are unlikely to internalise these, at least without overbearing transaction costs attaching. The externalities may take the form of pollution. Producers commonly utilise the environment to the point at which the costs of environmental degradation may exceed the benefit to consumers of the product, unless there is intervention to redress the market failure. Similarly, natural resources may be depleted at too great a rate if the cost of utilisation reflects only the direct cost to the user and not problems of future scarcity. Economists recognise such externalities and understand the need to intervene to effect a remedy, but it is undoubtedly true that, in practice, problems such as intergenerational equity have been inadequately addressed at a political level.

Quite how one might intervene to remedy externalities is a problem that continues to trouble policy makers. Certainly, it is possible to consider market solutions, in other words, to create a market that works efficiently to redress the negative forces of the externality. Anthony Hobley offers the example of the possibility of trading greenhouse gas emissions. To work, such a system, as with any market, will require a good number of players willing to trade permits, to avoid the danger of the effective monopoly of the system by a few powerful operators. As Anthony's paper shows, the system is complex, but too great a level of complexity might increase transaction costs and generate informational problems, so that, even if environmental emissions reduce, the solution may prove less than efficient. Moreover, although one can see that the idea of trading permits might control diffuse impacts of greenhouse gases, it does depend on State regulation in the form of imposed ceilings on emissions. These will need to be backed by strict control of the limits, and penalties will need to be set that exceed compliance costs, otherwise the system will fail. One is dependent, therefore, in constructing the market solution, on the support of the courts and it is to be hoped that their understanding of the regulatory process as a whole is sufficient to grasp the need for appropriate levels of fines. Indeed, in his paper, Mike Quint makes this point splendidly in considering the deterrent effect of penalties in providing the climate for effective quantitative risk assessment.

Note also that there will not always be room for this type of solution. It works much more easily where there are widespread and diffuse impacts rather than a localised and identifiable pollution source. In such a situation, unless one is minded simply to ban an activity, then the likely response of law will be to impose a liability rule. Coase[5] has argued that, in the shadow of a clear private law rule, the parties will bargain to produce efficient solutions to regulate the potential harmful activity. Allan Rickmann's paper offers some feel for this, demonstrating as it does the development of transactional devices to allocate risk in the light of the liability rule. In turn, this has led to an emerging market for specific insurance to then cover the risk undertaken. In a different way, Stephen Tromans' paper makes a similar point. If we have a planning system which allows landfill or other disposal facilities to be sited in proximity to residential areas, the permission will often express the hope that the environmental regulator will adequately control the activity so as to prevent a nuisance. As Stephen points out, the courts have tended to 'shy away' from the grant of an injunction. However, if the courts are unwilling to exercise their discretion to restrain the conduct that amounts to a nuisance, there is little room for the Coase bargain between the parties, leaving those affected adversely by the nuisance uncompensated. That these regulatory philosophies have a real world dimension is amply illustrated by the task presented by the need to diversify patterns of waste disposal in the manner outlined in Peter Kellett's paper, and demanded by the Landfill Directive

---

5   Coase, R, 'The problem of social cost' (1960) 3 Journal of Law and Economics 1.

(Council Directive 99/31/EC), in a situation in which people's experience of landfill produces stout opposition to the siting of waste facilities.

Peter Kellett's paper is an excellent review of a regulatory approach not primarily based upon market instruments, but on more public law based models of permitting potentially polluting activity subject to conditions. It is easy to see the introduction of qualities that should underpin that regulatory process, such as that the regime be flexible but holistic and that it work in an open and transparent manner. Under the Landfill Directive there are clear targets to work towards, but as Peter's paper demonstrates the regulation is detailed and complex. The issue for the economist then becomes the efficiency with which the benefits incorporated into the targets can be realised given the costs attaching to these forms of control. However, efficiency is not the only issue, since there may be distributional effects of different forms of regulation. Thus, instruments such as environmental taxation have the capacity to distribute money, especially when allowances such as landfill tax credits can be offset against the tax. We have seen in the discussion above that, although they attempt to evaluate advances in the common good, economists do not find it easy to provide practical analysis of the interrelationship between efficiency and advances in social welfare.

One problem that obviously presents itself in assessing environmental costs and benefits is that these are not easily quantifiable in terms of the types of market pricing mechanisms traditionally used as a measure by economists. Economists may attempt to gauge from behaviour quite how great a value one might wish to place upon less tangible benefits of (say) a clear sky unaffected by light pollution, but this is not an easy matter for empirical assessment. As Hilary Neal points out in her essay on biodiversity, this is a natural resource which is capable of utilisation, which ought to be valued and conserved for its benefits. However, the importance attaching to biological diversity is of recent origin and, in its nature, it consists of the interrelation of environmental resources. We know from the governmental response as described by Hilary that value is placed on biodiversity, but the quantification of that value is highly problematic. Moreover, of that value only a fraction will attach to that attributable to the future use of ecosystems. Much of the value has little to do with its use, but is intrinsic.

Here, in part, the problem is that it becomes difficult to fit public goods into a pricing framework. If goods are non-rival, and we can enjoy a clear sky or a scenic view without prejudicing the possibility of its enjoyment by others, then pricing based on market competition is hardly possible. Yet, the economist can hardly be blamed for trying to attribute value. At the heart of the endeavour is an attempt to examine what benefits are available at what cost. If the cost is to be measured in pounds, then the same unit of measurement is needed for the benefits to allow effective comparison. This is all very well providing that we remain conscious that we are engaged in a regulatory enterprise in which society is examining the best way in which to conserve that which is valuable. This is not an attempt to say that everything has its price in the sense of allowing the wholescale sale of our environmental birthright with total disregard for others elsewhere in time or space.

From an environmental ethics perspective, the extent to which one accepts at all this attempt to place a value on the environment is governed by underpinning notions of moral responsibilities in relation to the environment. This is because the exercise by the economist is implicitly anthropocentric, looking at choice as exercised by and value through the eyes of human actors. Human interest alone may be seen as driving environmental responsibility. This may be justifiable if we believe that only human beings have direct moral standing and that, as part of responsibility for the well-being of others, we ought to serve human interests by protecting the environment. One slight problem with this analysis is that if standing is accorded only by virtue of humanity, then responsibilities and rights should be accorded only to fellow human beings, by which we might mean only those with a present right to have their interest served and protected. This arguably rules out the rights of future generations, since why should people yet to exist be accorded rights any more than, say, any other creature not fixed with moral standing.

It is this type of argument that promotes arguments that moral significance should be extended beyond persons presently alive. For some, this would include at least some animals. If we accord moral significance to at least some animals, then, although we remain fixed with an indirect obligation to the environment – to protect it in the interests of others – a wider view is taken of environmental responsibility, since those others include (at least some) animals. None of this suggests a responsibility to the environment in its own right. This is the position advocated on an ecocentric view, although writers might disagree as to whether this accords the environment moral standing, or whether it is enough that the environment has some form of inherent value not fixed by human (or animal) activity, but deserving of respect and creating a duty.

Most famously, the relationship between ecocentrism and economics is found in Aldo Leopold's essay on the Land Ethic.[6] Propounding an ecocentric model of a widened community of interest – entitled the land and composed of soil, water plant and animal life – Leopold is critical of economics based approaches, even when some form of economic value is attributed to (say) plants or animals so that potential impacts upon them might be considered, because, in his view, they are entitled to consideration as a matter of biotic right. Thus, the economic mindset is the enemy of ecocentrism in promoting the environment as a commodity to be exploited by a human 'conqueror'.

---

6   Leopold, A, *A Sand County Almanac, and Sketches Here and There,* 1987, New York: OUP, p 204.

Leopold suggests a new moral principle of judging the rightness of action by whether it preserves the biotic community.

Many philosophers would reject such a consequentialist approach whereby the correctness of an action is to be judged by its effect, arguing in favour of a more deontological approach, whereby conduct or behaviour may be considered wrong from the outset as offensive to moral rules Indeed, in other circumstances, utilitarian approaches when judged by the overall welfare of humans might have no great appeal to those promoting environmental interests. Nonetheless, the importance of ecocentric approaches may be that, in positing the inherent worth or standing of the environment, they force a consideration of present modes of behaviour towards the environment and, in so doing, help promote changes in attitudes.

On this analysis, ecocentric approaches to environmental ethics have limited utility as a normative tool. The same comment was made earlier about environmental economics. This does not mean that either endeavour is worthless. Rather, the value of each lies in the positive analysis provided by each theoretical position. Within the UK Environmental Law Association (UKELA), which hosted the conference at which these papers were presented, members are interested in environmental regulation. Indeed, active groups within the association comment regularly upon policy proposals and environmental law reforms. A significant proportion of the membership consists of practitioners, whether lawyers or environmental consultants engaged in practical problems of pollution control. This allows an insight into the impact of policy proposals as they find their way into environmental regulation (although we can only rarely use the phrase 'onto the statute book' these days). But, how truly do we evaluate legal provisions and separate out effective reform as effective or ill-considered?

The simple truth is that we must look beyond law itself. If we do no more than weigh the latest judgment of the courts in terms of how consistently it matches earlier precedent, then we may develop a highly consistent common law (no bad thing), but one which is inward looking and treats law as an entirely autonomous entity existing in some juridical vacuum. The advantage of both environmental economics and environmental ethics is not that either of them should tell us what the law is, but that both of them offer a paradigm from which the workings of legal rules can be viewed. It is the capacity of these disciplines to ask some fundamental questions about the entire enterprise of environmental regulation that makes the exploration of them so valuable.

It might seem odd, therefore, that a conference attended by a majority of practitioners (the majority of these practitioners of law) should make the effort to explore wider questions of economics and of ethics. It is true that, as conference organisers, we did try to mix some of the more academic perspectives with papers of a more immediate practical input – lest we tested too greatly the patience of our audience on two fine June days in the year 2001 in Cardiff. Nonetheless, we are grateful to the UKELA Council for allowing us the freedom to bring together these papers and we hope that the debate that they created in Cardiff and their interest to the reader now promotes the fine tradition of UKELA as an organisation engaged in mixing a genuine interest in the environment with active debate on environmental policy.

CHAPTER 2

HAS ENVIRONMENTAL INSURANCE COME OF AGE?

Allan Rickmann[1]

DEVELOPMENT OF SOLUTIONS

Environmental insurance in the United Kingdom has grown rapidly in maturity, diversity and capacity in the past 10 years, mirroring the growth in environmental legislation. In areas where the law is undeveloped, damages and liability are difficult to establish. For example, with the introduction of the superfund legislation in the United States, new liabilities emerged. At that time, general liability policies in the US and UK did not recognise pollution as a potential liability and insurers did not collect premiums to cover the claims which emerged. This resulted in massive losses for the primary insurers and re-insurers and led to a retrenchment within the industry. In the US, general liability policies excluded all pollution based claims and, in the UK in 1991, the Association of British Insurers introduced the pollution exclusion into public liability policies. This excluded all claims for property damage and injury arising from pollution, except for cases where the pollution was sudden, accidental and unintended. So, by 1991 there was no insurance cover available in the UK for historically contaminated sites and for pollution which emerged gradually. The response from the insurance industry, and especially brokers, was to seek specialist environmental insurance to meet the needs of industry and commerce.

SPECIALIST ENVIRONMENTAL INSURANCE

Every year since 1990, new specialist environmental policies have emerged from insurers in the London market to introduce new products and add capacity. Occasionally, however, some insurers, like Reliance, have disappeared. Table 1, below, indicates how that growth has occurred.

---

1   Allan Rickmann has more than 20 years' experience in the fields of environmental protection and occupational health and safety and five years' experience in environmental insurance broking. He has sat on the Council of the Institute of Environmental Management and Assessment and on the Confederation of British Industry Environmental Affairs Committee. He can be contacted by email: rickmann@ntlworld.com.

Table 1: Specialist Environmental Insurers

Year	Specialist Environmental Insurer
By 1990	Swiss-Re
	AIG
By 1995	Swiss-Re
	AIG
	ECS
	Wallace Syndicate/Lloyds
By 2000	Swiss-Re
	AIG
	ECS/XL
	Wallace Syndicate/Lloyds
	Certa/Alliance
	Zurich
	RoyalSunAlliance
	Independent
	Chubb
	Kemper

LIMITS AND PERIODS

One of the limiting factors of the early environmental insurance policies was the upper limit of cover which was available and the periods over which the policy would operate. Table 2 illustrates how these parameters have changed over the past 10 years.

Table 2: Environmental Insurance Limits and Periods[2]

Year	Period	Limit of Cover
1990	3 years	£3 m
1995	10 years	£10 m
2000	25 years	£65 m

---

2   These are typical figures to illustrate the general point. There has always been more flexibility in the environmental insurance market than with other more mature types of insurance. So there has always been scope to stretch these parameters, as there is today.

DIVERSITY AND SOPHISTICATION

The discussion so far has been concerned with the insurance of the business risks primarily associated with historical contamination because that was the dominant environmental concern in the UK. However, over the past 10 years, a wide range of specific environmental insurance solutions has been developed and these are described below and illustrated with case studies. An important aspect of modern environmental insurance policies is that they are sufficiently flexible to meet business needs. The policy wording of almost every environmental insurance policy, of whatever type, is modified to suit the needs of the deal, the business partners involved and the circumstances. The specimen policies provided by all of the insurance companies are written as general documents relating to all circumstances and eventualities. Consequently, they contain many limitations, restrictions and exclusions, many of which are not relevant to the situation for which environmental insurance is required. The role of the broker is to represent the best interest of the client and design, with the underwriter and the client's legal advisers, the most appropriate policy wording and cover and negotiate a realistic premium.

The range of environmental insurance policies currently available address the following risks:

(a) historical contamination;
(b) environmental warranties and indemnities;
(c) future pollution;
(d) remediation cost management;
(e) contractors' pollution liability;
(f) planned expenditure risks.

INSURANCE SOLUTIONS

Historical contamination insurance

The type of environmental insurance most in demand in the UK over the past few years was probably that needed to cover the financial risks associated with historical contamination. To place this cover, the insurer will require sufficient information in the form of environmental survey reports to define the business risk. Where the site is a new development on agricultural land, a simple desktop survey may suffice. However, where there is a history of industrial activity, an intrusive survey is usually required. It is important to emphasise that the insurance addresses the business risk rather than the environmental risk. Policies have been placed where the site was legally contaminated, but where the circumstances or situation were such that the risk of enforcement action or third party civil action was unlikely.

Cover is available for periods of up to 25 years, although most insurance companies are more comfortable with policy periods of 10 years. Indeed, where longer periods are agreed, there are often clauses allowing the insurance company to revise the policy after 10 years to take into account any changes in the law. Only exceptionally are 25 year policies placed with no breaks. The limits of cover available are routinely £65 m, although higher limits have been provided.

An example of where historical contamination cover was effectively used to reduce financial risk was the redevelopment of a former steel works site. The steel works had been in production for more over 100 years, until the 1970s. During that period, substantial quantities of liquid wastes had been pumped into a deep coal measures aquifer. The environmental survey indicated that the aquifer was contaminated and was in hydraulic continuity with a river. This was clearly a contaminated site. However, there had been over 30 years of dilution and dispersion and natural biodegradation was continuing. The enforcement authorities took the view that the risk of harm was both low and reducing and that the contamination could not be cost effectively remediated and so no enforcement action was envisaged. Nevertheless, there remained a real and finite latent business risk and the developers and their funders wanted the long term financial situation secured. Historical contamination insurance was placed giving £10 m cover for 15 years for a one-off premium of £150,000.

Environmental warranties and indemnities

In 2000, most environmental insurance placed in the UK was related to historical contamination cover. However, more recently, there has been strong demand for insurance to cover environmental warranties and indemnities given during mergers and acquisitions. Clearly, the straightforward triggers used for historical contamination cover would not match the wording of most environmental indemnity agreements. Consequently, the cover developed has been written to respond directly to claims under the environmental indemnity agreement. Since this results in a much wider range of situations to which the policy will respond, the premiums are correspondingly greater. Nevertheless, since this type of policy fits well into the wording of sale and purchase agreements, many of these policies have already been placed.

This type of insurance has been used to good effect in several large scale voluntary housing stock transfers and is becoming a standard method of financial risk transfer in these transactions.

Future pollution insurance cover

These policies are variously called Environmental Operational Risk (EOR) or Environmental Impairment Liability (EIL). They are designed to provide the insured with financial cover for the costs involved in cleaning up the insureds own site or third party property in the event of a spillage or leakage or similar event where the cleanup is required by statutory notice. These notices would include enforcement notices, abatement notices, remediation notices and works notices. In addition, the policies will provide cover for the costs of civil claims from third parties for death, injury or property damage resulting from the pollution spillage or leakage. Generally, the legal costs of dealing with the statutory authorities and criminal and civil cases will also be met by the insurer.

To place this cover the insurer will require evidence of sound environmental management at the premises. Certification to ISO14001 or accreditation to EMAS is one of the criteria which insurers consider when assessing business risk. However, it is important to establish that not only does the company have a documented environmental management system, but the system is actively and effectively implemented. This is usually achieved by the submission of a current environmental audit report detailing the environmental performance of the operation. Cover is available for periods of up to five years. However, the insurance can usually be renewed on an annual rolling basis providing the insurer is satisfied that the standard of environmental management has been maintained.

Clearly, where the site or sites may have already been contaminated, it is necessary to place combined historical contamination and future cover.[3]

Remediation cost cap insurance

Site remediation cost cap cover is designed to ensure that the costs of remediation do not exceed preset and agreed limits. Specific site cleanup engineering works are designed and costed with contingency for reasonable overrun included. When these designs and costs are approved by the underwriter, site remediation cost cap insurance cover is available.

The insured organisation is committed to paying for the remediation engineering works with the insurer agreeing to pay any additional costs up to agreed limits. For instance, if a site remediation exercise is expected to cost £10 m, cost cap insurance cover may be obtained to provide cover for any

---

3   Eg, a European retail organisation concerned about environmental liabilities associated with 1,300 retail outlets placed cover for both historical contamination and future pollution. The cover had a £5 m limit with a deductible of £25,000 for three years, with a premium of £150,000.

additional costs, subject to the agreed contingency buffer, of perhaps £500, 000 up to a limit of £20 m.

This class of environmental insurance is designed specifically to cover major unexpected circumstances, such as undiscovered sources of pollution, rather than poor project cost estimating.

This type of policy is currently provided on a project specific basis and is available to site owners or occupiers and developers, but not remediation engineers, contractors or anyone involved in the project cost estimating process.

Contractors' pollution liability

Where environmental liabilities might arise, or be made worse, by contractors undertaking construction or engineering work, insurance can be provided for the contractors rather than the specific sites where the work is carried out. For example, poor management of on-site fuelling of construction equipment may lead to diesel contamination of the site and neighbouring land. The insurance would cover the costs of cleanup of the site and the third party land, any work required by the enforcing authority and legal defence costs. Similarly, where a contractor inadvertently creates a new pathway for contamination to slowly migrate from the site into, say, an aquifer, the insurance would cover the costs of remedial work and third party claims.

Planned expenditure management

Environmental insurance will only cover fortuitous issues for which an appropriate risk assessment can be carried out. It will not provide for unavoidable capital improvement expenditure which is required under statutory licensing regimes or other known or highly likely expenditure.

Finite risk funding solutions are currently available and are designed to take the timing risk out of such investment projects, to provide a financial cap on the costs and provide a tax-efficient investment vehicle. These complex risk financing deals are structured to address the unique requirements of each problem.

Recent changes to accounting procedures[4] tighten up the rules on when companies can make financial provision on their balance sheets for such potential expenditure, adding another risk factor, the impact on financial reporting, to the equation. Finite risk funding solutions can smooth the impact of this phenomenon.

---

4   Eg, Accounting Board of Standards, *Provisions Contingent Liabilities and Contingent Assets*, FRS 12, September 1998, amended September 2000.

An example of this type of deal is the provision of flue gas desulphurisation plant for power stations. European draft Directives indicated that this plant would be required some time in the future, but the timing of the investment was uncertain. The cost of the capital equipment would be £10 m and would be required some time in the next 10 years. Finance risk cover involved agreeing to pay an insurer £1 m per year for 10 years plus a premium. If the fund was required in, say, year two the insurer would provide the finance. However, if the cash was not required by the end of the 10 year period, the insurer would return the £10 m paid plus 95% of the investment income. The insurer would keep the premium plus 5% of the investment income.

CONFERENCE QUESTIONS

A delegate asked if I had any concerns about environmental solicitors placing environmental insurance directly with insurance companies, without going through a broker.

My response to the conference was to explain that environmental insurance brokers had a primary and legal duty of care to their clients. Environmental insurance brokers must provide their client with the best advice in terms of the economic stability of the insurance companies, the cover provided, the cost of the premium and the claims handling ability of the insurance company.

Insurance brokers check daily the financial rating of the main insurance companies they work with. Over the past five years, two major insurance companies that offered environmental insurance cover have failed. The brokers warned their clients, where possible, of the impending failures and replaced the cover for their clients with other insurance companies.

Specimen environmental insurance policies provided by insurance companies are general documents intended to cover a wide range of situations and circumstances. They, therefore, contain many exclusions, limitations and restrictions. These environmental insurance policies are often extensively modified by environmental insurance brokers, in consultation with the underwriters, to produce a final policy wording which best suits the client, the circumstances and the deal which the client is pursuing. Accepting an unmodified specimen policy wording will probably result in an inadequate level of cover.

Environmental insurance cover is always placed subject to detailed environmental survey reports. These reports describe the environmental impacts and risks associated with a site or company. In assessing the business risk, it is also important to consider the planning and enforcement implications. The broker must explain to the client that full disclosure of all material data, information and documentation is important. For instance, failure to disclose a letter from the Environment Agency expressing concern about a site may be sufficient grounds for an insurance company to attempt to cancel a 10 year policy.

Environmental insurance brokers work very closely with the environmental insurance companies arranging cover on a daily basis. Consequently, they are fully aware of the appropriate level of premium for any particular risk. The broker is, therefore, in a much stronger position than an environmental solicitor to negotiate a reasonable and proper level of premium.

In many cases, the environmental insurance broker will know from his experience which insurance companies will provide the best response to a given risk. For instance, some insurance companies are very concerned about undetected underground storage tanks, others avoid covering landfill sites, whilst others will routinely seek to exclude endocrine disrupters. The broker may, therefore, approach only two or three of the environmental insurance companies rather than the 10 available. The broker will then produce for the client a table comparing the extent of cover, exclusions, financial rating, and premium against the limit of cover required with particular deductibles. The broker will then provide an analysis of these factors and a recommendation of which insurance company offers the most appropriate cover for a given set of circumstances.

Going forward, the client will expect the broker to act on his behalf to notify him of any changes in the circumstances which will affect the policy and to manage any claims arising from the policy. Since many environmental insurance policies for historical contamination will remain in effect for 10 years, there could be several potential claims arising over that period. The broker acts on behalf of the client to negotiate with the insurance company to respond to the claim. The claim may be straightforward, or there may be issues of dispute arising from the interpretation of the policy wording. Most major brokers have claims management departments staffed by professional claims managers who are skilled at resolving these disputes without resorting to the courts. It is important for environmental solicitors, and, indeed, environmental consultants, to consider the duty of care they owe to their clients if they intend placing environmental insurance directly with insurance companies. Their clients have the right to expect that they will undertake the duties of the environmental insurance broker. Failure to discharge fully this duty of care may result in them attracting unexpected liabilities.

CONCLUSION

Environmental insurance can be considered to have come of age when it makes a positive contribution to the business cycle. Not only must it add value to deals when it is placed, but it must also be effective in responding to claims when it is called upon. Environmental insurance has certainly proved to be effective in facilitating deals, particularly mergers and acquisitions. Over the past three years, more than 500 environmental insurance policies have been placed in the London market. The income taken in insurance premium in the London market has doubled every year from £5 m in 1998 to an estimated £40 m in 2001. By contrast, the amount spent on environmental insurance premiums in the US is $1.3 bn. Environmental insurance will have truly matured in the UK when there is a demonstrable claims history. To date there have been six claims. One was outside the cover provided, two were settled within the deductible layer, one is currently in dispute and two are being evaluated by the underwriter prior to settlement.

The future trend is for environmental insurance to become integrated into normal property transactions as a versatile legal mechanism providing more effective protection for clients.

CHAPTER 3

IMPLEMENTING THE LANDFILL DIRECTIVE THROUGH THE PPC REGIME IN ENGLAND AND WALES

Peter Kellett[1]

THE ENVIRONMENT AGENCY'S LEGAL SERVICE[2]

The Environment Agency[3] (the Agency) is currently organised into eight regions[4] with a head office in Bristol. Some 70 legal staff are evenly deployed across this structure. Regional legal teams conduct prosecutions, provide advice on operational matters, conduct civil litigation and contribute to the national legal debate. The head office team provides strategic advice to policy functions[5] on new legislation, assists policy development and is increasingly involved in defending Agency decisions in national litigation.[6] Each policy function has a senior legal adviser.

The Agency's legal service convenes a number of national legal groups[7] that try to ensure consistent legal advice is given to both internal clients and, also, external stakeholders. Each group meets periodically to consider legal

---

1   Peter Kellett is a solicitor at the Environment Agency, Head Office, Legal Services Directorate, Government Offices, Block 1, Burghill Road, Westbury-on-Trym, Bristol BS10 6BF; email: peter.kellett@environment-agency.gov.uk. The views expressed in this article do not necessarily represent the views of the Environment Agency. Bridget Marshall assisted with this paper and is the Environment Agency's senior legal adviser and first point of legal contact on implementation of the Landfill Directive.

2   Whilst not strictly within the scope of this paper it may help UK Environmental Law Association delegates in their dealings with the Agency's legal service to understand a little of its structure.

3   Ie, the Environment Agency for England and Wales established by the Environment Act 1995, s 1. See www.environmentagency.gov.uk.

4   The seven regions and Environment Agency Wales are divided into 26 areas that are responsible for the operational delivery of the Agency's functions.

5   These functions currently include: radioactive substances regulation; water quality; water resources; fisheries; navigation; waste management and regulation; process industries regulation; and land quality.

6   Cases the legal services directorate has been involved in the last few months include: *R v Environment Agency ex p Emanuela Marchiori and the Nuclear Awareness Group* (High Court, 29 March 2001); *AG's Ref 5/2000* (Court of Appeal, Criminal Division, 4 May 2001); *Castle Cement v the Environment Agency* (High Court, Queen's Bench Division, 22 March 2001); *R v the Environment Agency ex p Mayer Parry Recycling Ltd*; and *R v Environment Agency ex p Anglian Water Services Ltd* (High Court, 27 October 2000).

7   Eg, a group meets to consider issues arising in prosecution and enforcement.

issues and form national views on some of the very complicated and difficult issues that concern the development of environment law.[8]

The Agency's legal service is instructed in all of its environmental litigation.[9] If you are instructed in any actual or pending litigation, please contact the relevant regional solicitor for the region in question[10] or the Agency's director of legal services[11] or their teams in the first instance, not other Agency employees.

Complaints and commendations are an important way for the Agency to improve its services. If you consider that the Agency has not provided the service you expect of a public body, then tell us.[12] There is a formal complaints procedure which you should follow.[13] Complaints will be investigated and treated seriously.[14]

INTRODUCTION

This paper considers the legal mechanisms though which some elements of Council Directive 99/31/EC of 26 April 1999 on the landfill of waste[15] (the Landfill Directive) will be implemented into English and Welsh law.[16] It considers how landfills will be permitted in future. The government signalled its intention to implement key requirements of the Landfill Directive in the Waste Strategy 2000 for England and Wales using powers under the Pollution Prevention and Control (PPC) Act 1999.[17] This intention was confirmed when the Department of Environment, Transport and the Regions (DETR) released

---

8   Many interests are considered in reaching a national view and this may take some time. Some external legal advisers regularly attempt to bypass this route to achieving certainty for their clients by cold calling various legal departments about 'hypothetical' situations.

9   This retainer is, of course, without prejudice to the rights of any person to access to environmental information and to information upon the public registers.

10 Again, see the Agency's website for addresses or dial the Agency's helpline on 08459 333 111. In an emergency, to report an incident call 0800 80 70 60.

11 Ric Navarro (see fn 1 for contact address).

12 The Agency employs many people who are genuinely committed to environmental protection and willing to respond to constructive criticism.

13 The complaints and commendations policy can be found on the Agency's website and in the Agency's customer charter.

14 Using the threat of making a complaint as a legal negotiating tactic simply because the position the Agency adopts is not favourable to the circumstances of a particular client is unlikely ultimately to benefit that client.

15 Ie, Council Directive 99/31/EC of 26 April 1999 on the landfill of waste published in the *Official Journal of the European Communities* (OJ L 182/1, 16.7.99).

16 I understand that separate regulations will be made in respect of Scotland and Northern Ireland.

17 Ie, the Pollution Prevention and Control Act 1999, Chapter 24.

its consultation paper on implementing the Landfill Directive[18] (the Consultation Paper) in October 2000. The Agency followed with a Second Consultation Paper in August 2001 but the United Kingdom was obliged to implement the Landfill Directive by 16 July 2001.[19] Transitional arrangements were put in place in the form of the Pollution Prevention and Control (Designation of Landfill Directive) Order 2001.

A separate consultation process is being conducted upon the Art 5 Landfill Directive requirements to reduce the amount of biodegradable waste going to landfill[20] and this issue is not addressed further in this paper.

THE POLLUTION PREVENTION AND CONTROL REGIME

The Agency sees the Pollution Prevention and Control Regime (the PPC Regime) as the future regime for environmental regulation. It will play a key role in delivering the Agency's Vision.[21] The PPC Regime marks a step change from the legislative controls on the landfill of waste under Pt II of the Environmental Protection Act (EPA) 1990.[22]

Reliance on secondary legislation

The PPC Regime is wholly reliant on secondary rather than primary legislation.[23] The Pollution Prevention and Control Regulations[24] (the PPC Regulations) contain the entire legislative framework and are the first regulations made under the PPC Act 1999. Regulations made under the PPC Act 1999 may applied, changed, or removed with comparative ease at a time

---

18 DETR, *Consultation Paper on Implementation of Council Directive 1999/31/EC on the Landfill of Waste*, 2000, London: DETR, Chapter 2, para 2.5.

19 At the time of writing (15 June 2001), draft regulations promised for consultation for early 2001 had yet to be published; see *op cit*, DETR, fn 18, Chapter 1, para 1.12. Note that the second consultation paper (*Implementation of Council Directive 1999/31/EC on the Landfill of Waste* available on the DEFRA website) was published in August 2001 following the UKELA Conference. The Second Consultation Paper is not addressed in this paper.

20 The reductions are set out against 1995 baseline values in Art 5, para 2 to the Landfill Directive: 25% within five years; 50% within 10 years; and 65% within 15 years. See the consultation paper entitled *Limiting Landfill October 2000 and the Waste Strategy 2000 England and Wales*, London: DETR.

21 Copies of the Agency's Vision are available from the Agency's website.

22 Ie, the EPA 1990, Chapter 43, Pt II (as amended) and the Waste Management Licensing Regulations 1994 SI 1994/1056 (as much amended).

23 Note the parliamentary safeguards that exist in the PPC Act 1999, ss 2(7)–(9).

24 The Pollution Prevention and Control (England and Wales) Regulations 2000 SI 2000/1973.

when Parliament may have little time for environment Bills. This has allowed minor changes and drafting corrections to be made.[25] More fundamental changes may also be made to the PPC Regulations.[26] Even without the Landfill Directive, it is likely that further changes will be made to the PPC Regulations in due course.

New concepts

The PPC Regime introduces new concepts and applies control to the 'operators' of 'installations'. It is necessary to consider these two concepts further.

Installation

The PPC Regulations apply define 'installation' to mean:

> (i) a stationary technical unit where one or more activities listed in Part 1 of Schedule 1 are carried out; and (ii) any other location on the same site where any other directly associated activities are carried out which have a technical connection with the activities carried out in the stationary technical unit and which could have an effect on pollution ...

At complex sites where multiple activities are carried out, defining the extent of the installation or installations is a complicated task and must be approached with care.[27] Some installations will be much larger than the individual units regulated under previous regimes. This might occur where an installation under the PPC Regime includes activities previously subject to regulation under separate environmental permits issued under Pts I and II of the EPA 1990. For example, a power station with a dedicated ash landfill may together form a stationary technical unit and so form one installation for which at least one PPC permit is required. How many permits are required for each installation depends on how many operators there are (see below). The number of permits also depends upon timing. Before phasing into the PPC Regime under the transitional provisions, an operator of an existing

---

25 Note the Pollution Prevention and Control (England and Wales) (Amendment) Regulations 2001 SI 2001/503 which correct minor drafting errors at reg 2(4), (5) and move certain activities from Pt B (air pollution) to Pt A(2) (integrated) regulation.

26 See the simplified system of control for mobile air curtain incinerators for use during the foot and mouth epidemic contained within the Pollution Prevention and Control (Foot and Mouth) (Air Curtain Incinerators) (England and Wales) Regulations 2001 SI 2001/1623.

27 Guidance upon the definition of installation is provided in *IPPC* [Integrated Pollution Prevention and Control] *a Practical Guide*, Annex II. The Agency will supplement this guidance in due course with a further regulatory guidance note which will be published externally in the interests of transparency.

installation may not make a substantial change in operation unless it has obtained a permit for that part of the installation affected by the substantial change.[28] It will need to apply for a second permit for the rest of the installation at the relevant time under the transitional provisions.

Operator

The PPC Regulations define the operator in relation to an installation as 'the person who has control over its operation'.[29] Under the PPC Regime, where more than one person controls different parts of an installation, each will require a separate permit. Under Pt II of the EPA 1990, it is possible for one person to hold a waste licence for a facility (perhaps a holding company or a local authority), but for another to operate that facility (perhaps a subsidiary company or a contractor). Under the PPC Regime, the regulator can only grant or transfer a permit to a person who will have control over the operation of the installation.[30] Should a permit holder lose control of an installation, then the regulator is also empowered to revoke the permit.[31] Applicants for permits will have to ensure that they fall within the definition of operator in future.[32] One consequence of this definition for the landfill industry is that, where separate legal persons have control over different parts of an installation, then more than one permit will be required to operate the installation. At some installations, therefore, one permit will be required for the waste disposal activity and another will be required for operation of the landfill gas equipment.

Flexible regulatory mechanisms

The PPC Regulations contain more flexible regulatory mechanisms that should cause regulatory control to be both focused and more proportionate than under the EPA 1990. New mechanisms allow the partial transfer[33] and

---

28 See the PPC Regulations, Sched 3, para 4.

29 See *ibid*, reg 2(1).

30 See *ibid*, regs 10(3), 18(4).

31 See *ibid*, reg 21(2)(b).

32 Note that an Agency regulatory guidance note to staff on the meaning of 'operator' will be published shortly and made available externally in the interests of transparency.

33 Cf EPA 1990, s 40 and the PPC Regulations, reg 18. Thus, a PPC permit holder can divest part of its assets to another person. Any attempt to use this mechanism for landfill liability avoidance should be prevented by the requirement of the proposed transferee of the transferred part of the permit to be a fit and proper person; see the PPC Regulations, reg 18(5).

partial surrender[34] of permits, an option that was not available under Pts I or II of the EPA 1990. Further, for the first time the regulator is able to consolidate permits.[35]

Openness and transparency

The PPC Regulations are more open and transparent than Pt II of the EPA 1990. For the first time, there is a requirement upon the proposed operator to place a statutory advertisement inviting public representations as a part of the decision making process.[36] The advertisement must not just describe the activities to be carried out, any foreseeable significant effects of emissions from the installation, and describe where the particulars of the application may be viewed, but it must also explain that written representations may be made to the regulator. Regulators must also refer applications to a much wider range of statutory consultees and take their comments into account in determinations.[37] The wider range of consultation responses may make decision making more complicated even before the requirements of the Human Rights Act 1998 are considered.

Enforcement mechanisms

The PPC Regulations contain enforcement mechanisms that need fresh consideration for those used to Pt II of the EPA 1990. Whilst there is little change in the powers of the regulator to serve enforcement notices,[38] the consequences of non-compliance with an enforcement notice under the PPC Regime have changed. Under the PPC Regime, there is additional criminal liability, but this will not lead to suspension of the permit unless the regulator considers that there is an imminent risk of serious pollution.[39] If such a risk exists, the regulator is under a duty to suspend the activities.[40]

---

34 Cf EPA 1990, s 39 and the PPC Regulations, reg 19; this should allow parcels of land within PPC installations to be freed up for better uses once they become redundant and have been returned to a satisfactory state.

35 This discretionary power should lead to more simple and transparent regulation, eg, where a permit has been amended a number of times the amendments can be consolidated into a single document that is simpler for all to follow.

36 See the PPC Regulations, Sched 4, paras 5 and 6. No such requirement exists within the framework of the EPA 1990, Pt II.

37 See the wide range of statutory consultees in the PPC Regulations, Sched 4, para 9.

38 Cf the EPA 1990, ss 42(5), (6) and the PPC Regulations, reg 24.

39 Under the EPA 1990, s 42(6), the waste regulation authority may revoke or suspend a licence where a licence holder has failed to comply with an enforcement notice but non-compliance with such a notice is not an offence and the notice cannot be appealed against; see the EPA 1990, s 43(1). Under the PPC Regulations, an enforcement notice can be appealed against; see the PPC Regulations, reg 27(2).

40 See the PPC Regulations, reg 25(1).

The Agency considers that the hurdle to suspend permits under the PPC Regulations for landfill may be set rather high. Operational control over the landfill process is much less direct than in other sectors and there is a considerable time lag between cause and effect which may lead to difficulty in establishing exactly when pollution is imminent.[41]

Sites reports and surrender

The PPC Regulations require applicants for permits to prepare an initial site report which must 'identify any substance in, on or under the land which may constitute a pollution risk'.[42] This initial report will be compared with a site report submitted as a part of a surrender application to identify any changes in the condition of the site as a result of the activities carried on at the installation. The PPC Regulations contain a surrender test that requires the regulator to be satisfied that appropriate steps have been taken to avoid any pollution risk and return the site to a satisfactory state.[43] This form of surrender requirement will be new to some activities subject to the PPC Regime, such as integrated pollution control under Pt I of the EPA 1990.[44] A surrender test is hardly a new concept to the landfill industry given the existence of s 39 of the EPA 1990.[45]

Regulatory package

The Agency consulted upon and produced a regulatory package to seek to ensure that a consistent and transparent approach is taken to regulation under the PPC Regime.[46] The regulatory package is available free of charge to applicants to assist them in preparing applications. It should help them

---

41 The Agency may have to consider the use of its other enforcement powers in such circumstances.

42 See the PPC Regulations, Sched 4, para 1(2)(s).

43 See *ibid*, reg 19.

44 Note that the *Fourth Consultation Paper on the Implementation of IPPC Directive*, 1999, London: DETR stated that the government would not accept a suitable-for-use standard for remediation under the PPC Regime as this would 'be to accept further significant degradation of the soil and land': see Pt 2, para 18.

45 Under the EPA 1990, s 39 licence holders must provide sufficient information to the waste regulation authority so that it can determine whether: '... it is likely or unlikely that the condition of the land, so far as the condition is the result of the use of land for the treatment, keeping or disposal of waste (whether or not in pursuance of the licence), will cause pollution of the environment, or harm to human health.' The PPC Regime test will be modified in the light of the Landfill Directive requirements on surrender, see below.

46 This package included standard application forms, an A(1) guide to applicants, the template permit, technical guidance and regulatory guidance notes to Agency staff on substantial change and the transitional provisions (which have been published externally in the interests of openness). Further guidance on the definition [contd]

provide sufficient information of suitable quality so that the regulator may make a timely determination.

The PPC Regime presents an exciting challenge to the Agency to move towards an integrated holistic regime and work cross-functionally. This has involved reprogramming IT systems, re-organising management systems and retraining sufficient staff to make determinations upon PPC applications.

By 1 June 2001, six permits had been issued by the Agency, 140 applications (including some 80 from the pulp and paper sector, the first sector to phase into the PPC Regime) had been received and some 230 pre-application discussions were in train with operators. This date also marked the opening of the window for a second wave of applications from the cement and lime sector to make applications for permits for continued operation.

IMPLEMENTING THE LANDFILL DIRECTIVE THROUGH THE PPC REGIME

The legislative graveyard for landfill regulation in the United Kingdom is extensive.[47] A landfill might have been licensed in 1993 under the Control of Pollution Act 1974, amended under Pt II of the EPA 1990, had part of its licence replaced under the PPC Regulations and will be fundamentally affected again by the pending Landfill Regulations.[48] Where landfills are poorly regulated there may be severe local impacts as the tragic case of *Floris Gertsen*[49] demonstrates.

Key requirements of the Landfill Directive include:

(a) statutory definition of landfill;

(b) the end of co-disposal of hazardous and non-hazardous waste in 2004;[50]

(c) pre-treatment requirements for waste to be landfilled;

---

46 [contd] of installation and on Sched 1 is in preparation. Over 1,000 points were raised and considered during this process.

47 See the Deposit of Poisonous Wastes Act 1972; the Control of Pollution Act 1974; and now for those landfills already caught by the PPC Regulations, the EPA 1990, Sched 1, para 5.2; and the Waste Management Licensing Regulations 1994.

48 Four regimes in less than a decade creates an uneven licence stock.

49 Floris Gertsen entered his garage accompanied by his dog to use his car. He turned on the ignition and immediately an explosion occurred destroying the garage, damaging the car and causing substantial injuries to his person. The explosion was caused by the migration of methane gas from the adjacent municipal landfill; see *Gertsen et al v Municipality of Metropolitan Toronto et al* (1973) 646 DLR (3rd) 41.

50 The term 'monofills' has been coined and, from July 2004, co-disposal will be banned; see *op cit*, DETR, fn 18, para 13.8 which provides: 'The Government's view is that co-disposal of hazardous and non-hazardous should end at all landfills by July 2004.'

(d) reductions in inputs of biodegradable waste to landfills;[51]

(e) increased waste recycling and recovery and hazardous waste treatment;[52]

(f) adequate provisions by way of financial security;[53]

(g) bans on certain waste streams such as tyres and liquid wastes;

(h) closure and aftercare for all landfills;

(i) technical requirements for matters such as leachate and landfill gas collection;

(j) Site Conditioning Plans to bring existing landfills up to standard;

(k) closure of sites that fail to meet those standards; and

(l) classification of sites into hazardous, non-hazardous or inert.

Complexity

A complicated system of landfill regulation arises from three key overlapping Directives: the Waste Framework Directive;[54] the Integrated Pollution Prevention and Control Directive (the IPPC Directive);[55] and the Landfill Directive. For example, each Directive requires that a system of permitting be put in place, but the activities that require a permit under each measure differ.[56] The overlap between the IPPC Directive and the Landfill Directive is addressed only in broad terms in the overall objective article of the Landfill Directive. Article 1(2) of the Landfill Directive provides: 'In respect of the technical characteristics of landfills, this Directive contains, for those landfills to which Council Directive 96/61/EC is applicable, the relevant technical requirements in order to elaborate in concrete terms the general requirements

---

51 See fn 20.

52 As ENDs has asserted the Landfill Directive marks a shift away from end-of-pipe waste management and: 'There has been alarmingly little discussion of what the UK's waste management system might look like after co-disposal is banned and curbs on biodegradables have been implemented'; see *Implementing the Landfill Directive: A Turning Point for UK Waste Management*, ENDs Report, Issue No 280, May 1998.

53 The requirement to make financial provision given the requirements of the EPA 1990, s 74(3)(c), is again hardly new to the waste industry.

54 Ie, Council Directive 74/442/EEC of 15 July 1975 on waste (as amended).

55 Ie, Council Directive 96/61/EC of 24 September 1996 concerning integrated pollution prevention and control (OJ L 257/26, 10.10.96).

56 The Waste Framework Directive requires a permit from the competent authority for amongst other matters the D1 operation 'deposit into or onto land (eg, landfill, etc)'; the IPPC Directive requires a permit for installations where listed activities are carried out including, Annex I, para 5.4, 'Landfills receiving more than 10 tonnes per day or with a total capacity exceeding 25 000 tonnes, excluding landfills taking inert waste' – unhelpfully neither the term 'landfill' nor the term 'inert' are defined in the IPPC Directive; the Landfill Directive (which incidentally does define 'landfill' and 'inert') contains requirements to create a system that applies to 'landfill permits'.

of that Directive. The relevant requirements of Council Directive 96/61/EC shall be deemed to be fulfilled if the requirements of this Directive are complied with.'

At the national level, the delivery of the Landfill Directive is particularly complex and will, the Agency understands, involve Landfill Regulations that will amend both the PPC Regulations and, also, Pt II of the EPA 1990 and contain self-standing provisions such as those relating to Site Conditioning Plans (see below) which are obligations outside the existing regimes.

A more complicated system of regulation is difficult to imagine.

What the English and Welsh system might look like

How the English and Welsh landfill regulation system could work was addressed in the Consultation Paper. The regime must work to deliver effective regulation during the transitional period.[57] In the absence of consultation draft Landfill Regulations at this stage, the following is based upon what is in the Consultation Paper and what may be required to make the system work effectively. The Agency would prefer that the new system, so far as possible, is grafted onto the PPC Regulations, so simplifying the number of regimes faced by industry and regulators alike and encouraging transparency for all stakeholders.

What the PPC Regulations already cover

Certain landfill activities are already covered by the PPC Regime as they were covered by the IPPC Directive. These activities are: '... [t]he disposal of waste in a landfill receiving more than 10 tonnes of waste in any day or with a total capacity of more than 25,000 tonnes, excluding disposals in landfills taking only inert waste.'[58] The Agency understands that this section will be widened on Landfill Directive implementation to include all landfills that are caught by the IPPC and Landfill Directives.

How landfills will fall subject to the PPC Regime

The transitional date for existing landfill installations that fall subject to the PPC Regulations and so must apply for a permit, under transitional rules, was

---

57 See text below on Site Conditioning Plans which describes how existing landfills may fall to be permitted.

58 The PPC Regulations, Sched 1, s 5.2, Pt A(1).

deliberately set at the back of the transitional timetable for the PPC Regime in 2007.[59] The Agency understands that this date will be brought forward on implementation of the Landfill Directive.[60] The Agency's preferred option is a rolling date which will be triggered by a requirement for the Agency to give an operator six months' notice before a PPC application is required. A rolling programme will be established on the basis of risk, that is, the more hazardous sites will be taken first.

Closed landfills

The Consultation Paper indicates that only those landfills that are closed before 16 July 2001 will avoid the requirements of the Landfill Directive.[61] Those sites will continue to be regulated under Pt II of the EPA 1990, for now. However, the government has consulted upon its ultimate intention to bring all Pt II of the EPA 1990 sites into the PPC Regime including such closed landfills.[62]

Phased applications and Site Conditioning Plans

The government proposes to bring landfills into the PPC Regime using a staged application process. Any site that fails to close before 16 July 2001 will have to submit a Site Conditioning Plan by July 2002. Site Conditioning Plans must include information on how the site will comply with the requirements of the Landfill Directive and any corrective measures to be taken to achieve this.

The Agency will ask operators to indicate in their Site Conditioning Plans whether they intend to close (that is, a recognition by operators that they will not reach the standards set by the Landfill Directive). Further, the Agency will seek to identify from the Site Conditioning Plans those sites that will *not* achieve the Landfill Directive standards. Sites that are identified to be closed at this early stage will not enter the PPC Regime but, instead, will be closed under an amended Pt II of the EPA 1990.[63] The rest of the sites will be phased

---

59 See the PPC Regulations, Sched 3, the table provides the window for such applications as 1 January to 31 March 2007.

60 See *op cit*, DETR, fn 18, para 2.4.

61 See *op cit*, DETR, fn 18, para 2.55.

62 See *op cit*, DETR, fn 18, para 2.56.

63 Precise figures are hard to predict as they depend in part on commercial judgments that may, in some cases, have yet to be made as to whether sites can economically meet Landfill Directive requirements, but it would be fair to say that a significant proportion of the smaller non-IPPC Directive landfills may face closure.

in on a rolling programme based on the risk they pose.[64] A consequence of the submission of a poor quality Site Conditioning Plan is that an operator may be required by the Agency to close its landfill.

The Agency will write to those sites that have not been identified for closure requiring the submission of a PPC permit application which corresponds to the rolling time programme described above. The PPC application will be largely based on the Site Conditioning Plan with the additional information required for a full PPC application. A failure to submit a good quality Site Conditioning Plan will mean operators will have to do more work at the PPC application stage. Government has indicated that all determinations should have been made by 2006 at the latest. It is envisaged that some requirements, such as bans on liquid waste and the requirement for pre-treatment, will apply from the date of the PPC permit determination. In other cases, each permit will contain an improvement programme setting out the required steps to bring the landfill up to Landfill Directive standards as soon as possible, but in any event by 2009.[65]

As soon as possible

For the purposes of the Landfill Directive, all improvements must be completed 'as soon as possible' and, in any event, by 2009.[66] The emphasis in the Directive is not upon placing each requirement upon the landfill industry to be achieved by 15 July 2009, but it is upon doing this rather earlier. The Agency will have to consider carefully the strategic implications of this requirement for its waste management function. What the Agency will do will depend, in part, upon what can be physically achieved and, also, upon the need to continue to direct resources towards non-landfill sites and enforcement.

Waste pre-treatment

Pre-treatment will be required for new landfills from July 2001, for existing hazardous waste sites from July 2004 and for other existing sites as soon as possible and by 2009 at the latest. The appropriate level of treatment, according

---

64 See *op cit*, DETR, fn 18, para 2.7.
65 See *op cit*, DETR, fn 18, para 2.8.
66 See Landfill Directive, Art 14, which requires Member States to take measures so existing landfills may not continue to operate unless improvements are accomplished as soon as possible and, in any event, within eight years of transposition of the Directive.

to the government, is 'that which can be reasonably undertaken in furtherance of the Directive's objectives (to protect the environment and human health). In considering the level of treatment required we consider that the environmental benefits of the treatment should be considered on balance, in accordance with the principle of proportionality'.[67] Waste producers will need to ensure that sufficient pre-treatment facilities are available to achieve this.

Classification

The Landfill Directive requires that hazardous sites are classified by 16 July 2002. The PPC permit will include a classification for each site as hazardous, non-hazardous or inert.[68] It is anticipated by the Agency that there will be relatively few inert landfills and a similarly small number of hazardous waste landfills or 'monofills'. The vast majority of landfills that remain in operation beyond 16 July 2001 are expected to be classified as non-hazardous. Various obligations flow from that classification, including bans on the acceptance of certain waste types and treatment requirements.[69] It is likely that the initial classification as hazardous in July 2002 does not necessarily mean that a site is permanently classified as hazardous. A Site Conditioning Plan may be able to indicate that a site will cease taking hazardous waste in 2004 and, thereafter, that it will intend to take non-hazardous waste. The PPC application will then be made for a non-hazardous site. This would allow a large number of sites to continue to take hazardous waste until 2004.

Lack of facilities for hazardous waste

The Agency anticipates that one consequence of the classification is that there will be limited void space for hazardous waste after 2002. The concerns of the Environment Agency are shared by industry. The Agency responded to the Consultation Paper on this issue as follows:

> ... the principal issue about ending of co-disposal is that of enforcement. The management of hazardous waste will be one of the biggest practical problems arising from implementation of the Landfill Directive, particularly since there is currently insufficient capacity nationally to deal with the wastes diverted from landfill. In our view industry is not likely to be able to make firm

---

67 See *op cit*, DETR, fn 18, para 6.7. The paper acknowledges that to avoid endless discussions between the Agency and waste holders, guidance is needed (para 6.8).

68 See Landfill Directive, Art 4.

69 See *ibid*, Arts 5 and 6.

decisions on, nor financial commitments to, additional waste treatment and disposal facilities until matters such as the waste acceptance criteria are confirmed. At this stage, the Agency thinks it is unlikely that sufficient additional capacity will be available by 2004, let alone 2002.[70]

Those companies that propose new long term hazardous waste facilities will no doubt face unprecedented public concern.

How conditions might be set

The Agency considers that the precise overlap between the requirements of the PPC Regulations and the requirements of Annex I of the Landfill Directive (see below), in whatever way it is incorporated into the proposed Landfill Regulations, will need careful consideration. One way to achieve a regulatory system that might work effectively would be to allow the Agency to meet the general requirements of both Directives by setting specific conditions via the use of the powers in regs 11 and 12 of the PPC Regulations. This is what the Agency has suggested.

Technical standards

The Landfill Directive also contains some concrete technical standards. It will be interesting to see what the government suggests (in its forthcoming consultation paper) that the Agency should do with such standards where landfill determinations are made after the due date for implementation, but before actual implementation.

One way of considering large parts of the Landfill Directive is as a technical standards document. For example, when you examine Annex I of the Directive[71] closely, two features are apparent. First, the annex was written by technical experts not lawyers.[72] Second, it mainly requires the exercise of discretionary judgment, rather than the imposition of prescriptive standards.[73] Annex I of the Directive might be considered in parts as similar

---

70 Environment Agency response to the Consultation Paper, Question 10: 'Views are invited from operators or existing co-disposal sites seeking to operate as non-hazardous sites on whether they would cease taking hazardous waste in 2002 or 2004.'

71 'General Requirements For All Classes of Landfills'.

72 This is not necessarily a bad thing as the knowledge of the engineering standards and methods is limited in the legal community, but it does lead to some curious drafting, such as that for recommended surface sealing at para 3.3 (which you will note on careful inspection is upside down).

73 In terms of discretionary judgment see, eg, the landfill location requirements in Annex I, para 1, and the continued use of words such as 'appropriate measures' (see paras 2 and 4.1), 'at least equivalent to ... the following' (para 3.2), and 'may be prescribed' (see para 3.3). In terms of prescription see, eg, the minimum standard that is set for permeability and thickness of the landfill base and sides by para 3.2.

to a BAT (best available techniques)[74] Reference note,[75] and is certainly not the whole story. It would not enable the regulator or an operator to understand the standards required for a site to operate without further guidance. One clear equivalent standard to BAT standards in Annex I of the Landfill Directive is the thickness and permeability of the landfill liner.

This new regime will need considerable supporting guidance. New guidance is needed from government, equivalent to *IPPC a Practical Guide*, for Landfill. The Agency will consult upon its draft regulatory package (including guidance on Site Conditioning Plans, classification and technical guidance) once there is a clearer understanding on how the government intends to implement the Landfill Directive.

Standard application form

As for the PPC Regime, the Agency will require the use of standard application forms so that the information received is in uniform format and contains the information that the Agency considers is reasonably required for the purposes of the determination.[76]

Fees and charges

The Agency is required to recover its costs from operators (in line with the polluter pays principle) through a charging scheme. The Landfill Directive is likely to require additional effort (for example, to consider Site Conditioning Plans for some 2,500 existing landfills) and the Agency will seek to recover those costs wherever possible. The Agency has stated that it: '... faces considerable additional work as a result of the [Landfill] Directive requirements, in particular for the existing 2,500 landfill sites in England and Wales. These new responsibilities are expected to impact over a similar time period to other new duties ... Phasing our workload is therefore essential to enable effective management of resource demands.'[77]

---

74 The PPC Regime aims to choose the best option available to achieve a high level of protection of the environment taken as a whole. It achieves this by requiring operators to use the best available techniques (BAT); see *IPPC a Practical Guide*, Chapter 9.

75 BAT Reference documents (known as BREF notes) are published by the European Commission on a rolling programme and based upon an exchange of information between Member States on BAT. The BREF notes will not contain any binding requirements, but Member States are to take account of them in their own determinations of BAT. Domestic guidance will be produced on the required standards and BAT for the individual sectors, drawing on the information contained within BREF notes.

76 A specific power will be required in the Landfill Regulations to require the submission of a Site Conditioning Plan.

77 The Agency's response to the Consultation Paper, para 2.10.

CONCLUSION

The Agency sees the PPC Regime as an ideal regime to help deliver its vision. The PPC Regime provides a more flexible and integrated regulatory system than Pt II of the EPA 1990. With a few reservations, the Agency welcomes the PPC Regime as the new home for landfill regulation, but full implementation is a challenge to the Agency given the:

(a) potential complexity of the potential regulations;
(b) interface with the PPC Regime (a new regime itself with new concepts such as 'installation'); and
(c) scope and timing of the task ahead.

The Agency would urge UKELA delegates to take the time to understand and comment upon the proposed Landfill Regulations.[78] In order effectively to implement the Landfill Directive, it is vital that the Landfill Regulations are clear and not unduly delayed; industry and regulators should be left in no doubt as to the standards to be applied and the domestic procedures for doing so. The requirements of the Landfill Directive should not be left to be decided by the Planning Inspectorate or the courts. The task of determining 2,500 landfill applications over a three year period is challenging enough.

---

78 See fn 19.

CHAPTER 4

CIVIL LIABILITY FOR LANDFILL SITES

Stephen Tromans[1]

INTRODUCTION

As a society we have become adversely sensitive to waste and its effects in a way which would seem incomprehensible to those who lived in any city in the UK a century ago. Waste is now something to be removed from households as efficiently and regularly as possible and, once removed, never to be seen or smelled again. It has become someone else's problem. After all, that's what we pay our council tax for, isn't it? It was not always so. Charles Dickens' novel, *Our Mutual Friend*, centres around a dispute over the ownership of 'the Mounds', Victorian examples of landraise by the deposit of refuse in central London.[2] Their proprietor, Nicodemus or 'Noddy' Boffin (otherwise known as the Golden Dustman), happily lives alongside them, in his house known as 'Boffin's bower'.

Introducing the villain of the piece, the wooden-legged Silas Wegg, to the Mounds, Boffin describes them in glowing terms:

> So now, Wegg, you begin to know us as we are. This is a charming spot, is the Bower, but you must get to appreciate it by degrees. It's a spot to find out the merits of, little by little, and a new 'un every day. There's a serpentining walk up each of the mounds, that gives you the yard and neighbourhood changing every moment. When you get to the top, there's a view of the neighbouring premises, not to be surpassed. The premises of Mrs Boffin's late father (Canine Provision Trade) you look down into, as if they was your own. And the top of the High Mound is crowned with a lattice-work Arbour, in which, if you don't read out loud many a book in the summer, ay, and as a friend, drop many a time into poetry too, it shan't be my fault.

---

1   Stephen Tromans is a barrister, 39 Essex St, a Visiting Professor at Nottingham Law School, and a council member of English Nature and is a trustee of Forum for the Future. He can be contacted by email: tromans@easynet.co.uk. A version of this paper appears in (2001) 13(4) Environmental Law and Management and we are grateful to the publishers, Lawtext (www.lawtext.com), for permission to reproduce the paper here.

2   The directions to the Mounds refers to a location off Maiden Lane.

Modern technology has changed the nature of rubbish, and the nature of its disposal. Mr Boffin's Mounds would almost certainly have been comprised substantially of ash from domestic grates, and would not have contained a single disposable nappy. The waste from a home today will contain a significant putrescible component and a whole variety of chemicals and plastics which would make sitting in a lattice-work Arbour atop it a less than inviting prospect. Compacted and transported in bulk, possibly hundreds of kilometres, it is deposited in strictly controlled sites equipped with industrial technology in terms of containment and gas and leachate control.

The modern reality is expressed by the chronicler of industrial America, Don DeLillo in his novel, *Underworld*.[3] There he describes one of the characters, Brian Glassic, an employee of the corporation Waste Containment Inc, who overshoots the freeway turn-off near Newark, New Jersey, and finds himself unexpectedly faced with a perspective of the massive Fresh Kills Landfill on Staten Island:

> Three thousand acres of mountained garbage, contoured and road-graded, with bulldozers pushing waves of refuse onto the active face ... It was science fiction and prehistory, garbage arriving 24 hours a day, hundreds of workers, vehicles with metal rollers compacting the trash, bucket augurs digging vents for methane gas, the gulls diving and crying, a line of snouted trucks sucking in loose litter ... The landfill showed him smack-on how the waste stream ended, where all the appetites and hankerings, the sodden second thoughts came runneling out, the things you wanted ardently and then did not. He'd seen a hundred landfills but none so vast as this. Yes, impressive and distressing. He knew the stench must ride the wind into every dining room for miles around. When people heard a noise at night, did they think the heap was coming down around them, sliding toward their homes, an omnivorous movie terror filling their doorways and windows? The wind carried the stink across the kill.

LANDFILL AND LIABILITY

Whilst the Landfill Directive and the National Waste Strategy dictate a large scale move away from landfill, there is no doubt that, for the foreseeable future, landfill will for many counties remain a major component of their waste management strategy. Last resort or not, as the handling of the foot and mouth aftermath demonstrates, when the chips are down landfill may be the only alternative to letting waste rot in the open air. Landfills will, therefore,

---

3   1998, London: Picador.

continue to have operational effects and closed landfills may, of course, give rise to environmental risks for decades. The concerns of affected local residents will, therefore, continue to require to be addressed. In *R v Leicestershire CC ex p Blackfordby and Boothorpe Action Group*,[4] local residents sought unsuccessfully to have quashed the grant of planning permission for the extraction of coal and clay and the disposal of 3.9 m tonnes of putrescible waste on a site near their homes. One of the residents, Susan Reiblein, described in evidence the noise and dust pollution experienced with the onset of mining operations, and the severe depression suffered as a result of anxiety that she would be unable to sell her house at a reasonable price or indeed at all. The house had been on the market for almost £170,000 in 1997, before the planning application was submitted.[5] With the mining and landfill operations taken into account, it was estimated to be worth anything between £82,500 and virtually nothing. By the time of the proceedings, she had abandoned the house and moved away from the area.

It may be argued that there are many modern projects which could have equally disastrous personal effects for those unfortunate enough to be living near them. Roads and airports may impact in terms of noise, sewage treatment works may give rise to odours, and so on. But there are concerns of a different order where major waste disposal facilities are concerned. There is the combination of possible effects, noise from huge vehicles, visual intrusion, unpleasant odours, extending over the active life of the landfill, maybe a decade or more. There is the fact that the waste will always remain there, giving rise to the 'dread' factor as to possible effects of long term exposure.[6] And there is the 'intrusion' factor, the feeling of unfairness of having to bear the burden of a facility which benefits others, those living miles away, out of the county possibly, whose rubbish is dealt with there.[7] Decisions under the planning system, based on utilitarian principles of what is the best solution for society at large, have great difficulty in addressing these issues. So, can civil liability provide an answer?

It is difficult to address the issues of civil liability for landfill sites without the context of statutory control. A landfill site today will be where it is because either the local planning authority or the Secretary of State gave planning permission for it. To what extent does that imply that its effects, in that location, must by definition be broadly acceptable? A landfill site today will be

---

4   [2001] Env LR 2.

5   There had been a previous, unsuccessful, application in 1996.

6   The psychological links between waste and desolation perhaps go quite deep: one of the words used in the New Testament for hell, Gehenna, was originally the valley of Ge-Himmon at Jerusalem, where child sacrifices took place, and which became the place for the burning of the refuse of the city, dead animals and the bodies of criminals. It was regarded as a fit symbol for the destruction of wicked souls.

7   For detailed discussion, see Gerrard, MB, *Whose Backyard, Whose Risk*, 1994, Boston: MIT.

subject to a detailed regime of control by the Environment Agency under the site licence and approved working plan. To what extent can it be assumed that such control will be exercised so as to contain environmental effects and environmental risks within acceptable limits, and within the parameters of the relevant objectives under EC law? Those objectives themselves illustrate the difficulty. Article 4 of the Waste Framework Directive[8] provides that among the objectives relating to the disposal of waste are that human health should not be endangered and that disposal should be without risk to the environment and should not cause nuisance through noise or odours. In planning terms, however, this has been held to have due regard to those objectives or to take them into account as material considerations.[9] Thus, the planning authority determines what weight to give to the avoidance of nuisance as against other material considerations and, ultimately, the issue is whether the likely degree of nuisance is acceptable in those terms.

CASE STUDY

These issues arose starkly in *Blackburn v ARC*,[10] where Mr Blackburn brought nuisance proceedings against ARC (trading as Greenways Waste Management) who operated a site near West Malling, Kent, close to his home. When Mr Blackburn bought his house in 1980 he was unaware of proposals to infill the nearby quarry with domestic waste, for which planning permission and a waste disposal licence were granted in 1981. By 1985, landfill operations began to intrude on the Blackburn family's life and, over a period until 1995, they experienced strong refuse and landfill gas smells, litter and noise. The judge found they were 'careful and conscientious and not prone to unnecessary exaggeration ... fundamentally tolerant and patient people'. Their evidence was not invented, contrived, or the result of over sensitivity. It was supported by numerous other local residents and visitors to their house. At the time the claim was heard, there was capacity for approximately 800,000 tonnes more waste in the site, which would generate revenue in the order of about £12 m. The defendant sought to rely on the fact that planning permission and a waste disposal licence authorised the relevant activities. This argument was rejected on various grounds.[11] For both planning permission and the site licence, the court would not allow an administrative decision to extinguish private rights without compensation. The operations, being of a temporary nature, were held not to have changed the character of the

---

8   75/442/EEC as amended by 91/156/EEC.
9   *Blackfordby v Boothorpe* [2001] Env LR 2; *R v Derbyshire CC ex p Murray* [2001] Env LR 26.
10 [1998] Env LR 469 (Official Referee's Business, HHJ Humphrey Lloyd QC).
11 See *Gillingham BC v Medway (Chatham) Dock Co Ltd* [1993] QB 343; *Wheeler v JJ Saunders Ltd* [1996] Ch 19.

neighbourhood for nuisance purposes. Also, the nuisances in this case were not inevitable. Perhaps most importantly, it was held that the fact that the planning permission and licence had been preceded by expert assessments of the likely effects did not prevent a finding of nuisance. The defendant also argued that the principle of reasonable user or 'give and take' between neighbouring occupiers applied.

The judge found that the use of the land in this case was not reasonable:

In my view it is quite clear that the use of land as a rubbish tip which will create smells and gas is not a reasonable user of land. If the smells and gas are more than that which must be tolerated in today's modern living conditions, the occupier of the land is liable in nuisance to adjacent owners.

I do not accept that it is reasonable to use land as a commercial rubbish tip which generates nauseating odours and gases.

But, in any event, the judge was not concerned with the tip as such, but with whether the defendant had, in operating it, caused nuisances. These activities considered over the years were held to fall well outside any latitude the law might allow. There was held to be nuisance from smell and from filthy litter being allowed to reach Mr Blackburn's land. However, much of the noise (from reversing beepers on vehicles and the flare stack) was held to be the inevitable consequence of the use of the site as a permitted tip and was disregarded in nuisance terms. There was no proven injury to health and damages were, therefore, assessed on the basis of the diminution in value of the property resulting from the nuisance (£25,000). Under the principles in *Hunter v Canary Wharf*,[12] it was held that it was not possible to award general damages.

Mr Blackburn also sought an injunction restraining the future operation of the site so as to cause a nuisance, given that the site was planned to operate for at least another three years. It was held it would not be appropriate to grant an injunction. First, it was emphasised that an injunction, though the primary remedy in nuisance cases, was a discretionary remedy. Damages were held to be sufficient compensation for the diminution in value. An injunction in relation to transitory nuisance, such as smell, would be difficult to police and enforce. A new flare stack was due to be installed which should improve the situation, and the judge felt it would be preferable to leave the control of litter and smells to the regulatory authority. However, Mr Blackburn was free to apply for an injunction should there be any repetition of past failures.

The decision raises some extremely interesting issues. Unfortunately, the judgment, whilst thorough and exhaustive in its evaluation of the factual evidence, leaves something to be desired in terms of clear exposition and application of the relevant legal principles. Some of these principles require further consideration.

---

12   [1997] 2 WLR 684, pp 698–99.

Authorisation by planning permission

The judge rejected the argument that planning permission could provide a basis for defeating claims in respect of nuisance that inevitably result from the development. Part of the reasoning here was that the planning permission – being for operations of a temporary nature – could not change the character of the neighbourhood.[13] However, he then suggested that if and to the extent that the claim arose out of activities which inevitably created a nuisance, the claim would fail. However, since in this case, the nuisances were not inevitable and were avoidable, they were not barred in law by the grant of permission or the licence. He went on to say that where the works would lead inevitably and unavoidably to smells and gas being released, the plaintiff would have to establish that the smells and gas constitute a nuisance in that they do not amount to a reasonable use of land. Whereas the smells could have been avoided (there were persistent mechanical or other failures in the venting system, and other instances of mal-operation), it was found that warning beeps from reversing vehicles on-site were unavoidable. Since much of the noise resulted from the inevitable use of the site as a permitted tip, this was excluded from consideration on the basis of *Wheeler* and *Gillingham*, which had been held earlier not to be applicable. The judgment, therefore, leaves the position somewhat confused, but, in any event, it is submitted that the issue needs to be addressed in rather wider contexts of remedies (see below).

Damages

The loss of amenity caused by the site was held to be foreseeable. In considering whether they had caused loss, it was not necessary to prove that a prospective purchaser had been put off buying the house by the smell and litter. It was sufficient if these factors were likely to affect the amenities and the value of the house. The judge stressed that damages for loss of amenity could not be assessed mathematically, but that did not mean they could not be awarded. In this respect, the decision of the House of Lords in *Hunter v Canary Wharf* was followed, in that amenity damage equated to a diminution of the value of land, even if its capital value was not affected.[14] The subsequent discussion centred entirely around conflicting expert valuation evidence. In an important section, the judge pointed out that the true difference in value attributable to the nuisance 'must exclude the very presence of a landfill site

---

13   Cf *Gillingham BC v Medway (Chatham) Dock Co Ltd* [1993] QB 343.
14   Hence, amenity damages are not affected by the number of persons living in the property.

... it is ... the permitted use and, following the reasoning in *Wheeler* and *Gillingham*, any diminution in value attributable to it should be disregarded as it has not been caused by the nuisances complained of'.[15]

Injunction

The injunction has traditionally been the primary remedy in cases of nuisance. As Buckley puts it: 'The injunction is the most powerful weapon in the armoury of the court in nuisance cases and is almost certainly the form of relief most commonly awarded.'[16] The judge found difficulties with Mr Blackburn's claim for an injunction restraining the carrying on of operations so as to cause a nuisance by smells. In particular, the nature of smells as transient meant that any such injunction would be difficult to police, and might lead to 'further troublesome proceedings'. Damages were felt to be an adequate remedy. It was felt that as smells and litter were matters for the waste management licence, it would be preferable 'to leave them to the regulatory authority'. There are some problems with this aspect of the judgment. The classic test in *Shelfer v City of London Electric Lighting Co*,[17] as to the award of damages in lieu of injunction, was not applied. The apparent faith in future control by the regulatory authorities has been cogently criticised:[18] '... one thing which this case does provide stark evidence of is the need for private law rights even in the context of a strict regulatory scheme.'

CONCLUSION

The case of *Blackburn v ARC*, therefore, points up the dilemmas involved in applying the common law of nuisance to regulated landfill activities.[19] The landfill as an activity in that location will have been authorised on public policy grounds by the authority which granted planning permission. It should be regulated by the Environment Agency in a way which prevents nuisance occurring to local residents. Failure to regulate it adequately – at least in sufficiently gross cases – may provide grounds for arguments as to liability on the part of the regulator, either on human rights grounds[20] or as a breach of EC law.[21] To grant an injunction for nuisance would – at least where the

---

15   [1993] QB 343, p 537.
16   Buckley, RA, *The Law of Nuisance*, 2nd edn, 1996, London: Butterworths, p 137.
17   [1895] 1 Ch 287.
18   See the Commentary to the case, [1998] Env LR 543–44.
19   For more general discussion, see Lowry, J and Edmunds, R (eds), *Environmental Protection and the Common Law*, 2000, Oxford: Hart.
20   *Lopez-Ostra v Spain* [1995] 20 EHRR 277.
21   *Francovich v Italy* [1993] 2 CMLR 66.

nuisance is inevitable – have serious implications for the public and would contradict the decision of the planning authority as to the acceptability of the site at that location. There is, therefore, an important public policy issue involved as to the exercise of discretion whether to grant an injunction, which (with certain exceptions, such as *Miller v Jackson*)[22] the courts have tended to shy away from.[23]

At the same time, an approach which denies any remedy for loss of amenity and diminution in property value (either because it is the inevitable consequence of the authorised activity or because it is due to the inherent presence of the facility) seems unjust. Why should the few people living downwind of a major landfill have to shoulder the burden of the disbenefits of a facility that serves the wider community? Indeed, is there not an argument that such effects, if uncompensated, could involve an unjustified interference with the relevant human rights? There is some hint of the courts recognising this issue in the cases dealing with the question of when common law rights are abrogated by statutory authorisation, in that the provision of a legislative scheme for compensation may give some indication that nuisance was regarded as inevitable and that the intention was to abrogate the common law rights.[24]

The siting of waste facilities promises to be one of the most contentious planning issues of the next decade. If current levels of public opposition to siting decisions are maintained, there is frankly little chance of the targets of the Landfill Directive being met. Is it not sensible to consider whether some form of compensation scheme may be possible for those communities affected by the presence of such facilities? To some extent this is happening already, through the allocation of landfill tax credit revenues by environmental bodies to local projects. There are signs that this is becoming a more scientific process, with allocation being influenced by the available information (for example, from the environmental impact assessment process) as to where the impacts are greatest in terms of lorry routes and meteorology. However, this can only go so far. There is, in my view, a case for monetary compensation of those affected, either by direct annual payments or by rebates from local taxes. In that way, the costs would be internalised and passed back in higher council tax bills to those whose waste causes the unsightliness, smells, noise and gulls which even the best run landfill site is likely to entail. If, at some point, such costs can be related to the amount of waste produced per household, so much the better. Nuisance is often said to be all about 'plain and sober and simple notions among the English people'.[25] Perhaps here is a chance to put such plain, sober and simple notions to effective use.

---

22 [1977] QB 966.
23 See Tromans, S, 'Nuisance: prevention or payment?' [1982] CLJ 87.
24 *Marriage v East Norfolk Rivers Catchment Board* [1950] 1 KB 284.
25 *Walter v Selfe* [1851] 4 De G & Sm 315, p 322.

CHAPTER 5

WHEN WILL THE LAWS PROTECTING DOMESTIC ANIMALS BE APPLIED TO WILDLIFE?

Mike Radford[1]

INTRODUCTION

The purpose of this paper is to consider whether our developing understanding of the factors which determine the quality of life experienced by other species has any implication for the way in which the law relating to wildlife may, or should, evolve. The emergence of animal welfare science as a distinct area of study and inquiry is relatively recent, dating from the 1960s, but it now has a very significant impact on public policy. In particular, it has informed and profoundly influenced the volume and nature of the legal protection afforded to domestic animals, in both British and European Community law.

By seeking to identify those factors which affect an animal's quality of life, the way in which it responds to its environment, and how successfully it is able to cope with the challenges which confront it, the focus of the law has begun to extend beyond simply seeking to prevent cruelty and unnecessary suffering. In many situations, it now also embraces a positive duty to promote a high quality of life for domestic animals. Giving effect to Council Directive 98/58/EC concerning the protection of animals kept for farming purposes,[2] it is now, for example, expressly required that owners and keepers take all reasonable steps to ensure the welfare of such animals under their care, having regard to: the species; their degree of development, adaptation and domestication; and their physiological and ethological needs in accordance with established experience and scientific knowledge.[3]

---

1   Mike Radford is based in the School of Law, University of Aberdeen. He is a member of the Council of the Universities Federation for Animal Welfare; Animal Welfare Science; Ethics and Law Veterinary Association and a member of the Companion Animal Welfare Council. He is also an academic advisor to and external examiner for the Royal College of Veterinary Surgeons. He can be contacted by email: m.radford@abdn.ac.uk.

2   Council Directive 98/58/EC, OJ L 221/23, 8.8.98.

3   Welfare of Farmed Animals (England) Regulations 2000 SI 2000/1870, reg 3(1)(a), (3); Welfare of Farmed Animals (Scotland) Regulations 2000 SSI 2000/442, reg 3(1)(a), (3); Welfare of Farmed Animals (Wales) Regulations 2001, reg 3(1)(a), (3) (the Welsh Regulations came into force on 31 July 2001, but at the time of writing had not been allocated an SI number).

It is self-evidently the case that the relationship humans have with the animals they keep as companions or for commercial purposes is fundamentally different from their relationships with those which are free living. First, where a person chooses to keep a domestic or captive wild animal, they can clearly be regarded as having voluntarily assumed responsibility for its care. Secondly, such an animal does not enjoy the same autonomy to satisfy its needs as its wild counterpart. Indeed, in many cases, its quality of life is determined entirely by the actions of its keeper. Nevertheless, it may be argued that the more we know about what is important to other species, regardless of whether they are living in a domestic or natural environment, the greater our responsibility to have regard to those needs.

TRADITIONAL DISTINCTIONS

Over a period of almost 200 years, there has grown up a voluminous and increasingly sophisticated body of legislation which lays down how domestic and captive animals are to be treated. In contrast, in so far as the law has been concerned to protect wildlife at all, it has generally focused on the conservation of specific types of animal considered to be at risk, or the protection of particular ecosystems and habitats.

This distinction between domestic and wild animals is deeply entrenched in the law. Historically, the issues concerning animals which came before the courts typically involved disagreements over ownership, or the rights and liabilities which might ensue from ownership. It is, therefore, not surprising that both English and Scottish common law defined the legal status of animals by reference to their standing as property. Hence, the courts distinguished between, on the one hand, animals which were domesticated or tamed, and could therefore be said to belong to someone, and those which were wild, and were owned by no one. 'In such as are tame and domestic (as horses, kine [cows], sheep, poultry, and the like) a man may have as absolute a property as in any inanimate beings,' Blackstone explained, 'because these continue perpetually in his occupation, and will not stray from his house or person, unless by accident or fraudulent entitlement, in either of which case the owner does not lose his property'.[4] In contrast, a person could not own absolutely a wild animal, although he might have qualified property in it where, for example, the creature had been lawfully taken, tamed, or reclaimed, but his property rights would be lost if the animal was released, escaped, or reverted to the wild.[5] Similarly, young wild animals were regarded as belonging to the

---

4 *Commentaries on the Laws of England*, 1765–69, 1979 edn, Chicago: University of Chicago Press, Book II, Ch 25, p 390.

5 *Case of Swans* (1592) 77 ER 435; *Blades v Higgs* (1865) 11 HL Cas 621.

person on whose land they were born, but only until such time as they were old enough to leave of their own accord; and a landowner had the right to hunt, take or kill wild animals while they remained on his land.[6]

Having defined the status of a domestic animal by reference to the concept of as being property, the courts were entirely concerned to safeguard the owner's rights in it; there was no regard for the animal's inherent needs. Accordingly, the owner of an animal might bring proceedings against a third party who had injured or abused it, on the basis that such conduct had reduced the animal's value, but the owner himself could (mis)treat it howsoever he pleased, and authorise his employees likewise, in exactly the same way that he could choose to do whatever he wished with his inanimate property. In 1809, Lord Erskine told the House of Lords: 'Nothing is more notorious than that it is not only useless, but dangerous, to poor suffering animals, to reprove their oppressors, or to threaten them with punishment.' 'The general answer, with the addition of bitter oaths and increased cruelty, is, What is that to you? – If the offender be a servant, he curses you, and asks if you are his master? and if he be the master himself, he tells you that the animal is his own.'[7]

Indeed, it was exactly the freedom to abuse – this 'defect in the law',[8] as Erskine described it – bestowed on the owners of animals by the common law, which provided the impetus for the introduction of the first animal protection legislation in 1822. Inspired by the routine and widespread cruelty meted out to horses in general, and to cattle while being driven to London from the country,[9] the 'Act to prevent the cruel and improper Treatment of Cattle', made it an offence for a person wantonly and cruelly to beat, abuse, or ill treat any horse, mare gelding, mule, ass, ox, cow, heifer, steer, sheep, or other cattle. This emphasis on the prevention of cruelty still forms the basis of animal protection legislation in Britain. Indeed, like a gene passed down the generations, the terms of that original measure remain extant. Thus, it remains an offence cruelly to beat, kick, ill-treat, override, overdrive, overload, torture, infuriate or terrify any domestic or captive animal, or wantonly or unreasonably do or omit to do any act which causes it unnecessary suffering.[10] The courts have held that the adverb 'cruelly' is, in this context, to be interpreted as applying to conduct which causes the animal unnecessary suffering.[11]

---

6   *Sutton v Moody* (1697) 91 ER 1063.
7   Parl Debs, Vol 14, col 554, 15 May 1809.
8   *Ibid.*
9   *Ibid*, for a contemporary description.
10 Protection of Animals Act (PAA) 1911, s 1(1)(a); Protection of Animals (Scotland) Act 1912, s 1(1)(a).
11 *Budge v Parsons* (1863) 129 RR 367; *Barnard v Evans* [1925] 2 KB 794.

In contrast to this concern for suffering, legislation relating to wildlife has, from the start, focused primarily on the preservation of species populations, not the treatment of individual animals. Hence, in 1869, a closed season for the killing of seabirds was introduced in response to the contemporary fashion for shooting them in huge numbers.[12] By means of further legislation introduced in 1872, 1876 and 1880, the category of birds protected during the breeding season was extended, first, to designated species of wild birds; then to wild fowl; and, finally, to all wild birds. In 1894, a further Wild Birds Protection Act empowered the Home Secretary to prohibit the taking or destroying of wild birds' eggs, either generally or in relation to particular species or within a specific area; two years later, powers were provided to confiscate the nets and decoy birds used by bird catchers; and, in 1902, the courts were given the power to confiscate birds and their eggs if they had been illegally obtained. While birds attracted such statutory attention, mammals were ignored, with the exception of the hare, whose population had declined dramatically because of the numbers being taken for food. The Hares Preservation Act 1892, therefore, prohibited their sale between March and July but, curiously, it remained lawful to kill them during that period.

WILDLIFE AND SUFFERING

Nevertheless, in specific contexts, Parliament has been prepared to introduce legislation which is clearly concerned to prevent or reduce the suffering of wildlife. For example, the Secretary of State may prohibit or restrict the use of a poison if he is satisfied that it cannot be used for destroying mammals without causing undue suffering, and an alternative method of killing them exists which is both suitable and adequate.[13] Further, it is an offence to use, knowingly permit to be used, sell, or possess a spring trap for the purpose of killing or taking animals, which has not been approved by the Minister of Agriculture, or to use a legal trap in circumstances for which it has not been approved.[14] Under the Wildlife and Countryside Act (WCA) 1981, it is also prohibited to use any springe (a noose or snare for catching small game), trap, gin, snare, hook or line, or any electrical device for killing or taking wild birds; and any trap, snare, electrical device or net in the case of named species.[15] It is

---

12 Sea Birds Preservation Act 1869.

13 Animals (Cruel Poisons) Act 1962, ss 2, 3. By virtue of the Animals (Cruel Poisons) Regulations 1963 SI 1963/1278, elementary yellow phosphorous and red squill may not be used for destroying mammals of any description and strychnine may be used only for destroying moles. Warfarin is specifically permitted, under prescribed conditions, to control grey squirrels: Grey Squirrels (Warfarin) Order 1973 SI 1973/744.

14 Pests Act 1954, s 8; see further the Spring Traps Approval Order 1995 SI 1995/2427; Agriculture (Spring Traps) (Scotland) Act 1969; Spring Traps Approval (Scotland) Order 1975 SI 1975/1722, as amended by SI 1982/92, SI 1988/2213 and SI 1993/167.

15 WCA 1981, ss 5(1)(a), (b) and 11(2)(a), (b); Sched 6.

a defence, however, to show that the article was used in the interests of public health, agriculture, forestry, fisheries or nature conservation and all reasonable precautions were taken to prevent injury to wild birds or protected animals.[16] The same legislation makes it an offence to set or use a self-locking snare calculated to injure, or for the taking or killing of, any wild animal.[17] Any spring trap set for catching hares or rabbits must be inspected by a competent person at reasonable intervals, but at least once every day between sunrise and sunset. Similarly, a snare must be inspected at least once every day.[18] In England and Wales, a spring trap may only be set elsewhere than in a rabbit hole, if it is used in accordance with regulations made by the Minister of Agriculture or the terms of a licence granted by him.[19] The WCA 1981 also prohibits other forms of taking and killing wild birds and animals, such as the use of any bow or crossbow, any explosive other than ammunition for a firearm, and any form of artificial lighting, mirror or dazzling device.[20]

In addition, two species which have been the subject of particular persecution are protected. The Conservation of Seals Act 1970 restricts the way in which seals may be killed and imposes a closed season on killing grey or common seals, and a complete ban on killing, injuring, or taking these animals at any time in English territorial waters has been introduced subsequently.[21] Except as permitted by statute, it is an offence wilfully to kill, injure or take a badger, or attempt to do so, or to interfere with a badger sett.[22] Cruelty to a badger is also expressly prohibited, which includes cruel ill-treatment, the use of badger tongs, or unlawfully to dig for it.[23]

Most significant, however, in extending the principle that wild animals should not be exposed to unnecessary suffering is the Wild Mammals (Protection) Act 1996 which, except as expressly permitted by the Act, makes it an offence to mutilate, kick, beat, nail or otherwise impale, stab, burn, stone, crush, drown, drag or asphyxiate any wild mammal with the intent to inflict unnecessary suffering.

---

16 *Ibid*, ss 5(4) and 11(6); Sched 6. See also Conservation (Natural Habitats, etc) Regulations 1994 SI 1994/2716.

17 *Ibid*, s 11(1)(a), (b).

18 PAA 1911, s 10; Protection of Animals (Scotland) Act 1912, s 9; WCA 1981, s 11(3) as amended by the Wildlife and Countryside (Amendment) Act 1991, s 2.

19 Pests Act 1954, s 9.

20 WCA 1981, ss 5(c) and 11(1), (2).

21 Conservation of Seals Act 1970; Conservation of Seals (England) Order 1999 SI 1999/3052.

22 Protection of Badgers Act 1992, ss 1, 3, 6 and 7.

23 *Ibid*, s 2.

THE CONCEPT OF WELFARE

While the prevention of unnecessary suffering continues to be the cornerstone of animal protection legislation in Britain, this test merely defines the standard below which conduct towards animals becomes unlawful. It imposes no requirement to improve upon that basic benchmark. Importantly, it fails to direct how animals *ought* to be treated. In consequence, it has been found that it relation to domestic and captive animals, focusing exclusively on unnecessary suffering is not, in itself, sufficient to protect them from inappropriate treatment, since there are many ways in which their standard of care may be less than satisfactory without it amounting in law to an offence of cruelty. It is, therefore, significant that there has evolved, especially since the end of the 1960s, a separate, but complementary, body of legislation, the effect of which has been to extend the legal duty we owe to domestic and captive animals, beyond simply ensuring that they are not treated cruelly. Increasingly, it now also embraces an obligation specifically to have regard to their welfare.

It is, of course, self-evident that the prevention of cruelty and the promotion of high standards of welfare are not discrete objectives. It is not surprising, therefore, that concern to prevent 'unnecessary suffering' is common to both strands of legislation; but while the legal definition of cruelty is defined almost exclusively by reference to this concept, welfare legislation also includes terms such as 'without suffering',[24] 'shall not be harmful',[25] and 'unfit'.[26] Such wording ousts the balancing exercise inherent in the 'unnecessary suffering' test, with the result that *any* suffering, harm, or injury may amount to an offence. Equally, an animal is either unfit or it is not; there is no requirement to consider the necessity of its condition. Furthermore, unlike the Protection of Animals Acts, welfare legislation may expressly require that those who care for animals positively 'prevent' or 'protect' them from suffering,[27] or take appropriate steps 'to avoid injury and unnecessary suffering and to ensure the safety of the animals'.[28]

Potentially the most significant feature of welfare legislation is, however, the introduction of criteria which are no longer defined exclusively by reference to suffering. For example, there are circumstances in which it is incumbent on those responsible to ensure the 'proper care and well-being' of

---

24 Animal Health Act 1981, s 40(2)(b).
25 Welfare of Farmed Animals (England) Regulations 2000 SI 2000/1870, Sched 1, para 11; Welfare of Farmed Animals (Scotland) Regulations 2000 SI 2000/442, Sched 1, para 11; Welfare of Farmed Animals (Wales) Regulations 2001, Sched 1, para 11 (see fn 3, above).
26 Welfare of Animals at Markets Order 1990 SI 1990/2628, Art 5(1).
27 *Ibid*, Arts 11(1) and 17(2).
28 Welfare of Animals (Transport) Order 1997 SI 1997/1480, Sched 1, para 1.

animals,[29] 'their health and welfare',[30] or their 'physiological and ethological needs';[31] others where a duty is imposed 'to maintain them in good health, to satisfy their nutritional needs and to promote a positive state of well-being',[32] or 'to safeguard the welfare of the animals under their care'.[33] On the face of it, this is regulation of a significantly different order from that which has traditionally prevailed. Rather than being concerned with whether the treatment of an animal has fallen below the rudimentary threshold of unnecessary suffering, provisions of this nature would seem to focus, instead, on identifying and meeting the innate needs of the animal itself.

WELFARE AND WILDLIFE

'Welfare' is an imprecise term; although it is now widely used in legislation, it is nowhere defined. Indeed, it is really a scientific concept, rather than a legal one. Despite the vagueness of its meaning, the idea of promoting welfare has been widely adopted. Perhaps, most significantly, in symbolic terms (if not necessarily in practice) is the fact that, by virtue of the Treaty of Amsterdam, a Protocol on Animal Welfare has been appended to the Treaty of the European Community which requires that: '... [i]n formulating and implementing the Community's agriculture, transport, internal market and research policies, the Community and Member States shall pay full regard to the welfare requirements of animals, while respecting the legislative or administrative provisions and customs of the Member States relating in particular to religious rites, cultural traditions and regional heritage.'[34]

It is unsurprising that, to date, concern for the welfare of animals has focused primarily on those creatures for which humans have direct responsibility. However, attention is beginning to turn to the welfare considerations of wild animals. For example, there appears to be general consent that. when there is a major oil spill it is entirely appropriate to catch and clean as many animals as possible, especially birds, which have been adversely affected. This is so, notwithstanding that they may be members of a species which is very common, and the number of individuals which

---

29 Zoo Licensing Act 1981, s 4(3).

30 Animals (Scientific Procedures) Act 1986, ss 6(5)(b), 7(5)(b).

31 Welfare of Farmed Animals (England) Regulations 2000 SI 2000/1870, reg 3(3); Welfare of Farmed Animals (Scotland) Regulations 2000 SSI 2000/442, reg 3(3); Welfare of Farmed Animals (Wales) Regulations 2001, reg 3(3) (see fn 3, above).

32 *Ibid*, Sched 1, para 22.

33 Welfare of Animals (Transport) Order 1997 SI 1997/1480, Art 9(1).

34 The European Court of Justice has recently given consideration to the meaning and application of the Protocol in Case C-189/01 *Jippes and Others v Minister van Landbouw, Natuurbeheer en Visserij*, 12 July 2001 (ECJ).

eventually will be released successfully back into the wild will have little or no benefit for the ecosystem. Similarly, where once a wild animal which was found to be sick or injured would normally have been either killed or left to die, it is now common practice for such animals to be 'rescued' and treated, with a view to their rehabilitation as free living individuals. As well as treating wildlife casualties at its establishments around the country, the RSPCA has, for example, three 'wildlife hospitals', equipped to a very high standard, which deal (almost) exclusively with non-domestic animals, and there are many other establishments around the country run by various organisations which perform a similar function. Furthermore, this type of work is now recognised as a distinct area of expertise within the veterinary profession.

There may be a legitimate debate about how worthwhile this work is, both in terms of its purpose and its success. It cannot be denied, however, that there is a significant body of opinion which takes the view that we have a moral duty to intervene to safeguard the welfare of at least some wild animals (as opposed to simply leaving them alone to get on with their lives as best they can). What distinguishes this attitude from a more general concern for the environment is the focus on the subjective experience of the individual animal, regardless of its rarity (or otherwise) or, indeed, its contribution to the well-being of the environment.

This is more than a side issue; as we have seen recently, and will probably see again soon, it has the potential to find its way onto the centre of the political stage. Here is not the place to consider the arguments for and against the practice of hunting with hounds, but questions about the welfare of the fox, individually and collectively, are clearly at the heart of the debate. Similarly, the National Trust introduced a ban on stag hunting on its land as a direct result of research which suggested that the effect on the stag of the chase was extremely detrimental to its welfare. Internationally, concern about the degree of suffering inherent in the use of the leghold trap led to an international dispute, with threats of a challenge under the WTO, when the European Union attempted to ban the import of furs caught using that particular method. Similarly, meetings of the International Whaling Commission regularly reveal a fundamental difference in approach between those delegations which consider that regulation of whaling should be restricted to protecting populations of species, and others which argue that the effects of hunting methods on individual animals are also a legitimate concern.

CONCLUSION

Although our relationship with free living animals is fundamentally different from those we have domesticated or keep in captivity, it is incontrovertible that human activity can have a profound effect on their quality of life. It is not surprising, then, that it is being argued by some that, 'if it is accepted that high standards of welfare should be a guiding principle in the husbandry of production animals, then it is inconsistent not to apply this principle to man's interactions with wildlife'.[35]

---

35 Sainsbury, AW, Bennett, PM and Kirkwood, JK, 'The welfare of free living wild animals in Europe: harm caused by human activities' (1995) 4 Animal Welfare 183–206. See also Kirkwood, JK, Sainsbury, AW and Bennett, PM, 'The welfare of free living wild animals: methods of assessment' (1994) 3 Animal Welfare 257; Harrop, SR, 'The dynamics of wild animal welfare law' (1997) 9 Journal of Environmental Law 287; Harrop, S and Bowles, D, 'Wildlife management, the multilateral trade regime, morals and the welfare of animals' (1998) 1 Journal of International Wildlife Law and Policy 64.

CHAPTER 6

ENFORCING BIODIVERSITY: A UK AND EU PERSPECTIVE

Hilary Neal[1]

INTRODUCTION

'Biodiversity' is a modern construct. As many of you will know, it is the portmanteau shorthand for 'biological diversity', coined first in 1986 by Walter Rosen and elevated to the level of international treaty in the Convention on Biological Diversity signed at the UN Earth Summit in Rio de Janeiro in 1992. Biodiversity signifies the variety of life on earth in all its forms. Such variety encompasses species, habitats and whole ecosystems. The Convention explicitly deals with humankind's interrelationship with biodiversity in terms both of its conservation and, also, of its exploitation and the sharing of the benefits of its exploitation, for example, with indigenous people. Thus, the convention seeks to articulate the view that biodiversity is a natural resource which may be utilised by people for their well-being and economic growth and that it must, therefore, be valued and conserved for the benefits it can bring to human beings, as well as for its own sake. At the time of the Earth Summit, the Biodiversity Convention took its place among the family of international treaties signed at that time as a central plank in the platform of sustainable development.

In using the term 'biodiversity', we consciously engage with the philosophy I have described. Until very recently, it had not appeared in formal legislation. Interestingly, Chapter 5 of Professor Ludwig Kramer's recently published *EC Environmental Law*,[2] is entitled 'Biodiversity and Nature Conservation'. Thus, he employs the modern terminology, but 'biodiversity' is referred to substantively only in the introduction to this chapter in relation to the Community Biodiversity Strategy, which has no legal force.[3] Setting aside the animal welfare community laws which are, familiarly but still oddly,

---

1   Hilary Neal is acting head of the European Wildlife Division of the Department for Environment, Food and Regional Affairs. Prior to this position, she was responsible for the implementation of the Natura 2000 aspects of the EC Habitats and Birds Directives. She can be contacted by email: hilary_neal@detr.gsi.gov.uk. The views represented here are her own and not those of the Government.

2   Kramer, L, *EC Environmental Law*, 4th edn, 2000, London: Sweet & Maxwell.

3   Biodiversity is also mentioned in passing with respect to the Zoos Directive (99/22/EC).

included under this heading, the legal provisions discussed in Professor Kramer's chapter relate exclusively to the conservation of species and habitats through site designation and protection and through control of human actions – such as disturbance, collection, trade, and hunting – over certain species, which could be damaging to their conservation status. The flagship European Union (EU) nature conservation laws are the Wild Birds and Habitats Directives and the CITES Regulations. These legal provisions might be considered to be the continuation of a traditional approach to nature conservation which has developed in the post-war period, but which the Biodiversity Convention has subsumed within its broader vision. So, let us look more closely at some of these specific provisions and return a little later to the concept of 'biodiversity' and whether it is enforceable.

LEGAL PROVISIONS

In the United Kingdom, the National Parks and Access to the Countryside Act 1949 first established a system of protection for designated Nature Reserves. These sites still are managed principally for nature conservation purposes or research. Because ownership is either by the State or by bodies approved by the conservation Agency and governed by nature reserve agreements, the question of enforcement of conservation in these areas barely arises, unless it be through control, by means of bylaws, of the activities of third parties or members of the general public who visit the sites.

A more ambitious approach to site conservation arose with the passage of the Countryside Act 1968, where the statutory predecessor to English Nature could enter into management agreements with private owners or occupiers of land that was of special interest for flora, fauna or geological or physiographical features (SSSIs). This was followed, in 1981, by the Wildlife and Countryside Act (WCA) that for almost 20 years provided the cornerstone for nature conservation in Great Britain. The WCA 1981 continued to pursue the management agreement approach following SSSI notification. The Act built up a complex procedure of notification of potentially damaging operations, which the landowner or occupier had to discuss with the statutory Agency before they could be undertaken, and financial arrangements whereby the landowner/occupier could be compensated for the profits which he or she would forego by not undertaking the operation. The arrangements for site protection relied on the voluntary principle whereby the owner or occupier would eventually agree to the terms of a management agreement, if necessary after the imposition of a Nature Conservation Order preventing the damaging operation from being undertaken while the negotiation period was prolonged. Eventually, however, where agreement could not be reached or the price of agreement was too high, the conservation Agency was unable to enforce the ban unless it could make out a case for compulsory purchase in the national interest. This uneasy equilibrium was maintained for many years and was largely successful in preventing most cases of outright damage to SSSIs by private land managers, but, because it was ultimately unenforceable except through compulsory purchase order (CPO), it was famously described as 'toothless' by Lord Mustill in *Southern Water v NCC*.[4]

And this approach failed to take account of some of the most significant causes of loss of biodiversity on these sites. One of these was development pressures, including public projects such as road building. Historically, planning guidance gave considerable weight to the SSSI designation as a material consideration in determining planning applications. However, it was not until Planning Policy Guidance 9 on nature conservation was issued in 1994 that it was suggested that certain SSSIs were sufficiently precious for developments significantly affecting them to be normally called in for the Secretary of State's own determination. Even in the case of Special Protection Areas under the EU Wild Birds Directive, DOE Circular 27/87 allowed that 'planning permission should be granted only where the authority is satisfied that disturbance or damage will not be significant ... or that [it] is outweighed by economic or recreational requirements'. This general approach was eventually considered to contravene the Birds Directive by virtue of the ECJ's ruling in the *Leybucht* case.[5] Subsequently, the EU Habitats Directive was to allow developments which would affect the integrity of such sites to proceed only on the grounds of 'overriding public interest' and only then if compensatory measures were provided. But, the increasing weight of planning guidance discouraging developments adversely affecting protected areas, together with public pressure in individual planning inquiries – whilst not formally amounting to a 'presumption against' – has gradually reduced the number of incidents of SSSIs damaged by development.

Another significant cause of biodiversity loss on protected sites is through simple neglect.[6] The site protection approach that simply guards against damaging operations, as in the WCA 1981, cannot contend with the decline which ensues from simply failing to undertake these management operations. So, the recently enacted Countryside and Rights of Way Act 2000 for the first time introduced the possibility of making a management order which requires the owner or occupier to undertake certain operations if the normal negotiations to reach a positive management agreement break down. It remains to be seen how often it will prove necessary to make such orders, but

---

4   [1992] 1 WLR 775.

5   Case C-57/89 *Commission v Federal Republic of Germany* [1989] ECR III-2849.

6   Most land of nature conservation value in the UK is special because of the type of management that it has traditionally undergone. Grazing by sheep or cattle is an important conservation tool which requires the right density of stock to maintain the interest. In other areas, meadows have to be mown at certain times of the year and, in heathland and woodland, active management is needed to sustain the diversity of the habitat.

they are expected to be rare. The Act also aimed to give teeth to the provisions preventing damage to sites by introducing a simple consent regime by English Nature, with penalties for non-compliance.

IMPLEMENTATION AND EFFECTIVENESS OF LEGAL PROVISIONS

The European Birds and Habitats Directives, adopted in 1979 and 1992 respectively, both applied the traditional approach to site and species protection of which we had had considerable experience in the UK. The UK, with its existing network of SSSIs and good management relationships with landowners and occupiers of those sites, has been well placed to implement the Habitats Directive's requirement to contribute to an EU-wide network of designated sites known as Natura 2000. But the rigidity of the Directives' provisions contrasted with the more flexible, voluntary approach traditionally applied in the UK. The implementing regulations, The Conservation (Natural Habitats, etc) Regulations 1994 had, therefore, to ensure that clear duties were placed on Ministers and the statutory conservation agencies to use their available powers (which would include CPOs) to ensure that the conservation status of the sites was maintained. The regulations also had to incorporate the Directive into the land use planning system, amongst others, to remove the discretion for local planning authorities to approve projects that were damaging to sites unless, in the Directive's words, they were needed for 'imperative reasons of overriding public interest'.

It is no exaggeration to say that Member States have found these two Directives amongst the most difficult and controversial of the EU environmental instruments to implement. Statistics published by the Commission show that over 50% of environmental infringement cases in the last 10 years have related to these two Directives alone. Infringement cases have ranged from those relating to the control of hunting provisions in the Birds Directive to specific site related cases providing test cases for the Directives' general provisions,[7] and so called horizontal actions for failure to transpose or designate sufficient sites. In Finland, it is said that the Habitats Directive gave the first opportunity for a mass public movement to be formed

---

7   *Santona Marshes Case*; Case C-355/90 *Commission v Spain* [1993] ECRI-4221; and *Lappel Bank* (1996) – see *R v Swale BC ex p RSPB* (1990) *The Times*, 11 April; *R v Secretary of State for the Environment ex p RSPB* [1997] Env LR 431 (HL); [1997] Env LR 442 (ECJ).

against nature conservation. It is interesting to reflect that Member States were still prepared to adopt the Habitats Directive by unanimity in 1992,[8] even after the problems they had experienced with the 1979 Birds Directive – though it has to be said that the Habitats Directive did sweep up and improve some of the more unsatisfactory elements of the Birds Directive. And governments across the EU have remained largely committed to implementation of the Directives, even though they have caused them untold difficulty in practice.

Most countries in Europe have been used to designating nature reserves and national parks where strict protection was maintained largely in publicly owned areas. Site designations would not be made where they could get in the way of economic development. The Directives, on the other hand, required designations to be made strictly on the grounds of their nature conservation value and successive case law in the European Court of Justice has reiterated this point, most recently in the case brought by First Corporate Shipping[9] in relation to the Severn Estuary. This has meant that large areas of private land in the EU which are under economic management or control must be designated and maintained in good conservation condition. The Commission estimates that by the time the Natura 2000 network is complete some 10% of the territory of the EU will be included. Member States have struggled to find mechanisms for ensuring that the agricultural land that comes within the designations can be managed sustainably for nature conservation and have grasped the possibilities offered by agri-environment schemes. And the European Commission has encouraged Member States and their populations to regard the Natura 2000 network as an opportunity to demonstrate sustainable development in action – where human activity interacts with nature in a mutually reinforcing way. Human activities are not precluded in these areas and even developments which might appear on the face of it to conflict fundamentally with the conservation objectives of a designated site can often be allowed to proceed by looking carefully at alternative locations, techniques or mitigation measures. The Commission has issued an unprecedented interpretation manual for Member States for the application of Art 6 of the Directive, which has no legal status, but which helps to guide practical decisions. Flushed with success, the Commission is now considering issuing something similar in relation to the hunting provisions of the Birds Directive, which is an even more controversial endeavour, if that is possible!

---

8   Under the pre-Maastricht regime for environmental instruments.

9   Case C-371/98 *First Corporate Shipping v North Somerset Council* [2001] EWCA Civ 693; *R v Secretary of State for the Environment, Transport and the Regions ex p First Corporate Shipping* [2001] 1 CMLR 19.

In respect of the Birds Directive, Professor Kramer concluded that it had had positive effects after 20 years. Compared with the soft law of international conventions, it had been successful in alerting administrations, public opinion and research to the state of bird life in Europe through the fact that the Commission had actively enforced and co-ordinated its provisions. However, his pessimistic conclusion was that it had, nonetheless, failed to stop the decline of wild birds in western Europe.

This conclusion is undoubtedly true. The relative inadequacy of such instruments as the Council of Europe's Bern Convention to enforce its provisions, compared with the Directives is evident. For example, the convention has spent the past 15 years discussing files relating to the problems of the encroachment of tourism on the turtle nesting beaches in Greece. Moral pressure on the Greek Government has been applied to take enforcement measures, but to no avail and the Standing Committee was forced to concede that it was no longer worth keeping the file current, especially since the Commission had opened an infringement procedure against Greece on this issue. Enforcement measures under the Habitats Directive, with its ultimate sanction of financial penalties, are much more likely to be successful.

But the broader conclusion that the overall decline in species has not been stopped is also true and remains worrying after so many years of effort in the nature conservation field. One is tempted to conclude that the approach has been too narrowly focused on strict protection of species and designated sites, and insufficiently on the wider ecosystems of which they are part. Apart from the species which are included in various lists as globally threatened or endangered in Europe, some once common species are subject to alarming declines. The populations of skylarks, for example, while still high at over 1 m in the UK, have declined by over 50% in the past decade. The populations of starlings and house sparrows have declined noticeably in recent years for, reasons which are as yet unknown – although we are carrying our research to find out the reasons. One is led to the conclusion that the problems of biodiversity loss are so intrinsic to the way developed society works that the traditional methods of site and species protection through legislation and its enforcement merely place the finger in the dyke.

Which is why the approach adopted by the Convention on Biological Diversity is so relevant and, in fact, so difficult. The convention acknowledges the importance of the traditional approaches to nature conservation but, also, insists that biodiversity conservation must be integrated through all areas of policy affecting human behaviour in order to stem the flood of species decline. It is axiomatic that the EU's Common Agricultural Policy has been the single biggest cause of species and habitat decline in the Community, closely followed by the Common Fisheries Policy. The fundamental policies of these instruments must be adjusted if the EU collectively is to live up to its responsibilities as a contracting party to the convention. In recognition of this fact, the Council adopted conclusions on an EU Biodiversity Strategy in 1998 and the Commission, under the strategy, has just adopted and published four sectoral action plans on agriculture, fisheries, natural resources and international co-operation and development which seek to identify steps towards more sustainable policies across the board in these fields.

This policy integration approach aims to apply biodiversity conservation across a broad front and requires fundamental shifts in behaviour and expectations, rather than compliance with narrow conservation laws. The manifestation in law of this approach would, thus, be through the legal instruments, or even fiscal measures which deliver the sectoral policies themselves.[10] It is similar to the UK's approach in its own Biodiversity Action Plan which not only lists the habitats and species for which particular conservation action is necessary, but also identifies the areas of policy and the necessary measures, such as water and forestry management, to tackle particular examples of decline. But, even here, the role of legislation to enforce biodiversity conservation is developing. During the passage of the Countryside and Rights of Way Act 2000, it was argued that a provision should be introduced to give a statutory basis to the UK Biodiversity Action Plan. This gave rise to s 74 of the Act which placed general duties on government Ministers and departments to have regard to the purpose of biodiversity conservation in accordance with the provisions of the convention, and on the Secretary of State to list species and habitats of principal importance for biodiversity conservation and take steps to further their conservation. Thus, the aims of the Convention on Biological Diversity are, to some extent, enshrined in law in England and Wales and the government has declared that this is an underpinning of the current UK Biodiversity Action Plan approach. Since these are very general provisions, the question of enforcement is an interesting issue that will no doubt develop as time goes by.

CONCLUSION

In conclusion, I believe that the direction that has been taken by nature conservation (or biodiversity) policy and law reflects the great complexity of the task. The idea that it is possible to preserve sites and species in isolation from the surrounding environmental, social and economic context is

---

10 Eg, in terms of conditions for receiving certain types of grant or subsidy.

increasingly untenable. And other factors, such as the impacts on biodiversity of climate change (which we know we are unable to reverse in the short to medium term, regardless of adherence to Kyoto targets) argue for a more holistic and dynamic approach to conservation in the landscape as a whole.

CHAPTER 7

THE UK EMISSIONS TRADING SYSTEM: SOME LEGAL ISSUES EXPLORED

Anthony Hobley[1]

INTRODUCTION

As a part of its Climate Change Programme,[2] the United Kingdom plans to be one of the first countries in the world to set up a fully functioning greenhouse gas (GHG) emissions trading scheme (ETS). To enter the scheme companies had to register their interest between July and September 2001. Having done so, if they wish to proceed, they must submit bids in January 2002 for total emissions reductions over a five year period against a baseline of aggregate emissions over the three years from 1998–2000. In return, successful bidders will earn up to a 10% share of a £215 m government incentive. However, the incentive is classed as a State aid under European Union (EU) law and so the government will require European Commission approval before the scheme can go ahead.

However, the UK is one of the few country's which is actually on course to achieve its targets under the Kyoto Protocol. Thus, the UK could choose to wait and, perhaps, learn from the mistakes of others. It has, instead, chosen to press ahead with its own scheme, even though this will at first, before 2008, have no clear legal basis under either international law or, for that matter, domestic law.

Inherent in this approach is the risk of putting in place systems that may turn out to be incompatible with those developed internationally. However, by being among the first countries to set up a fully functioning ETS, the government clearly expects economic advantages for the UK, its businesses and the City of London, which it believes will be well placed to play a leading and influential role in the development of such schemes internationally.[3] Business seems to share this view, since the form of the proposed ETS owes much to the initiatives of business itself, as discussed later.

---

1 Anthony Hobley is a senior solicitor with Baker and McKenzie, and Secretary to the UK Environmental Law Group and chairs the Emissions Trading Group Legal Liaison Sub-group on Compliance and Governance. He can be contacted by email: hob.mail@virgin.net.

2 DETR, *Climate Change, The UK Programme*, 2000, London: DETR (www.detr.gov.uk).

3 *A Greenhouse Gas Emissions Trading Scheme for the United Kingdom Consultation Paper*, 2000, London: DETR (www.detr.gov.uk).

The process of designing an ETS capable of delivering both real emissions reductions and an efficient market in emissions allowances is not as simple as it may at first appear. It is a considerable challenge, considering that the UK is ahead of the game and so will need to solve many issues for itself. In this context, it is clear that the government has set itself a tight timetable.

CURRENT POSITION

The government published its proposals in its Draft Framework Document in May 2001. The previous Consultation Document, published November 2000, had promised a full set of rules by May 2001.[4] The Department of the Environment, Transport and the Regions (DETR) decided that discretion is the better part of valour and that a full set of rules was not a realistic option within such a short timescale. In many respects, the Draft Framework Document is not a framework at all – it has more in common with a white paper than, for example, an EU Framework Directive or a piece of framework legislation.

This paper seeks to address some fundamental questions, such as why use emissions trading, introduce the basics of emissions trading and, then, examine some of the lessons learned, in practice, from the more than 20 years of experience of emissions trading in the United States. It will then address certain aspects of the proposed UK ETS, such as the eligibility criteria for entry; interaction with the Climate Change Levy (CCL); the functions of the registry; the nature of allowances and trading; enforcement; other sources of credits; and possibilities for international trading. However, to begin with, it will be useful to summarise briefly the international aspects of this issue, so as to put the UK proposals into context.

INTERNATIONAL PERSPECTIVE

The international community has slowly, and at times grudgingly, begun the long process towards building effective international and domestic measures to tackle GHG[5] emissions in response to the increasing certainty that global warming is happening and the uncertainty over its likely consequences.

That process began in Rio in 1992, when 160 countries agreed the UN Framework Convention on Climate Change (UNFCCC). The UNFCCC is, as

---

4   For the Framework Documents, see www.detr.gov.uk/climatechange/ tradingscheme.
5   Carbon dioxide, methane, nitrous oxide, hydrofluorocarbons, perfluorocarbons and sulphur hexafluoride.

its title suggests, simply a framework; the necessary detail was left to be settled by the Conference of the Parties (CoP) to the UNFCCC.

In 1997, the CoP agreed, in what has been described as a watershed in international environmental treaty making, the Kyoto Protocol where 38 developed countries[6] committed themselves to targets and timetables for the reduction of GHGs.[7] These targets for developed countries are often referred to as Assigned Amounts. The UK's target is to reduce its emissions of GHGs by 12.5% against 1990 levels by the Kyoto commitment period, 2008–12. The UK is one of the few countries likely to achieve its target and has, in fact, set itself a domestic target to reduce emissions of CO_2 by 20% against 1990 levels by 2008.[8]

One important economic reality recognised by many of the countries that signed the Kyoto Protocol is that, if countries have to rely solely on their own domestic measures, the resulting inflexible limitations on GHG growth could entail very large costs, perhaps running into many trillions of dollars globally over this century.[9] As a result, international mechanisms which would allow developed countries flexibility to meet their targets were included in the Kyoto Protocol. The purpose of these mechanisms is to allow the parties to find the most economic ways to achieve their targets, such as buying parts of assigned amounts (PAA) from other Annex 1 countries who have overachieved their targets, or funding the transfer of cleaner technologies to developing countries in return for credits to be counted towards their Assigned Amount.

There are four such international flexible mechanisms, or Kyoto Mechanisms,[10] written into the Kyoto Protocol. Article 17 of the Protocol authorises Annex 1 countries that have agreed to emissions limitations to take part in emissions trading with other Annex 1 Countries. Article 4 authorises such parties to implement their limitations jointly, as the Member States of the EU have chosen to do. Article 6 provides that such Annex 1 countries may take part in joint initiatives (JIs) in return for emissions reduction units (ERUs) to be used against their Assigned Amounts. Finally, Art 12 provides for a

---

6   Annex 1 countries.

7   Grimeaud, D, 'An overview of the policy and legal aspects of the international climate change regime' (2001) 9(2) Environmental Liability 39.

8   See above fn 2.

9   Stewart, R, 'Economic incentives for environmental protection: opportunities and obstacles', in Revesz, R, Sands, P and Stewart, R (eds), *Environment Law, the Economy and Sustainable Development*, 2000, Cambridge: CUP.

10   Yamin, F, Burniaux, J-M and Nentjes, A, 'Kyoto Mechanisms: key issues for policy makers for CoP-6; international environmental agreements (2001) 1 Politics, Law and Economics 187–218.

mechanism known as the clean development mechanism (CDM),[11] under which Annex 1 countries may invest in emissions limitation projects in developing countries and use certified emissions reductions (CERs) generated against their own Assigned Amounts. In this article, we are primarily concerned with how the Kyoto Protocol and, in particular, Art 17 are driving the development of a domestic ETS in the UK.

However, while the Kyoto Protocol provided for these flexible mechanisms, it did not set out the detailed rules which would govern how these would work in practice. This was to be left to subsequent CoPs. It was hoped that the outstanding issues would finally be settled at CoP-6 in The Hague. As we now know, this did not happen. However, contrary to much of the rather negative press coverage, significant progress was made on many of the detailed rules for the flexible mechanisms. It is also the case that CoP-6 did not end, but was suspended. Therefore, despite some of the abortive discussions after CoP-6, there is still room for optimism that a deal will be struck, but most likely without US support.[12]

Many of the negotiation texts for the flexible mechanisms are publicly available[13] as is the President of CoP-6, Dutch Environment Minister, Pronks, consolidated negotiation text and proposal.[14] These texts offer an extremely good outline of how the flexible mechanisms are likely to work in practice, thus providing a template for countries such as the UK to finalise their own schemes so that they are likely to be compatible with any future international schemes. The momentum in the UK is now such that, even if CoP-6 is unable to reach agreement, the UK is almost certain to press ahead on this basis.

WHY EMISSIONS TRADING?

The atmosphere is a dynamic air mass, subject to no national boundaries, and which cannot usefully be regulated as if it were land or territory. The status of the 'global atmosphere' under the rules of international law have yet to be settled and it is not clear whether it constitutes a shared resource, common property, common heritage or common concern or interest.[15] The 1985 Vienna Convention for the Protection of the Ozone Layer, for example, provides a model for treating the atmosphere as a global unity, whose the problems affect all States in common and whose integrity all States are required to

---

11 Haites, E and Yamin, F, 'The clean development mechanism: proposals for its operation and governance' (2000) 10 Global Environmental Change 27–45.

12 (2001) *The Independent*, 15 July, p 1.

13 See www.unfccc.de; http://cop6.unfccc.int.

14 See *ibid*.

15 Boyle, AE, 'Remedying harm to international common spaces and resources: compensation and other approaches', in Wetterstein, P (ed), *Harm to the Environment*, 1997, Oxford: OUP.

protect from harmful activities. The 1988 UN General Assembly – Resolution 43/53 declared that global climate change was 'the common concern of mankind'. One possible interpretation of the legal effect of this resolution is that it gives all States a legal interest, or standing, in the enforcement of rules concerning the protection of the global atmosphere.[16]

Whatever the status of the global atmosphere in international law, most commentators will agree that it is important to begin to consider it as a global resource which has an intrinsic value which, until now, has been regarded as zero. Perhaps the best way to conceptualise this intrinsic value is to consider it in terms of the global atmosphere's ability to absorb or carry greenhouse gases, such as carbon dioxide, without undue or detrimental effects on the earth's climate.

One way in which the global community or individual sovereign States can regulate this capacity is to set limits, or caps, on the total amount of greenhouse gases which can be emitted into the atmosphere. In effect, this is what the international community has attempted to achieve though the Kyoto Protocol by giving each of the developed or Annex 1 countries an emissions target. Each individual country can seek to meet its national target by imposing targets on individual entities and sectors within its own economy, such as individual industrial plants, power stations or whole sectors, such as the transport sector.

Under an emissions trading system, emissions sources must meet a set emissions target, but will have flexibility with regard to how they meet the target. An individual facility may purchase emissions reduction credits or allowances from other sources, sell credits or allowances, implement cost effective internal emissions reductions, or use a combination of both. This flexibility allows firms to use the most affordable compliance strategy, given their internal marginal abatement costs and the market price of allowances or emissions reductions or credits. In theory, a firm's individual decisions should then lead to an economically efficient allocation of reductions and lower compliance costs for individual firms and for the programme overall, relative to more traditional command and control mechanisms.[17]

---

16 *Ibid.*
17 Hall, JV and Walton, AL, 'A case study in pollution markets: dismal science US. Dismal reality' (1996) XIV Contemporary Economic Policy 67.

WHAT IS AN EMISSIONS TRADING SYSTEM? THE BASICS

Described in its simplest form, an emissions trading system will consist of a number of participants, each of whom will have a cap, or limit, on their total emissions over a specified period of time. The cap will have been set by reference to the total emissions for a particular participant over a specified period of time, often referred to as its 'baseline', which is used as a reference point for future emissions reductions. Within a classic 'cap and trade' trading scheme, participants take on caps, or targets, requiring them to reduce their emissions and, in return, receive allowances equal to their individual caps. Participants can choose either to meet their cap by reducing their own emissions; to reduce their emissions below their cap and, perhaps, sell the excess allowances; or to let their emissions remain above their cap, and buy allowances from other participants. All that matters is that, when it comes to demonstrating compliance, every single participant holds allowances at least equal in number to its quantity of emissions. The result should then be that the total quantity of emissions will have been reduced to the sum of all the capped levels.

If an emissions trading system is to be any more sophisticated than a series of bilateral trades, it will need to have a registry and a set of rules for organisations engaging in the system. The registry will, in effect, be a database which records the existence of the participants and the level of their cap and subsequently monitors the actual emissions and the trades that have taken place.

The rules of such a scheme would need to be transparent and broadly acceptable to all stakeholders. Issues that need to be covered include the method of determining baseline emissions from the participant and how emissions are to be monitored and verified against each participant's baseline. The reporting of baselines and emissions should be verified by external and accredited auditors. An effective penalty mechanism will be critical to deter participants from failing to meet their obligations. Governance of such a system will, therefore, be a major issue.

LESSONS LEARNT: THE US EXPERIENCE

The principle of trading emissions has been successfully demonstrated elsewhere, particularly in the USA, where markets in sulphur oxides and nitrogen oxides have been operating in some form for over 20 years.[18]

---

18   See p 62, above.

Before the sulphur dioxide Acid Rain Programme (ARP) was introduced into US law in November 1990, the US already had nearly 20 years of experience of emissions allowance trading, much of which was encapsulated into the US Environmental Protection Agency's (EPA) Emissions Trading Policy of 1986.

The history of the EPA's Emissions Trading Programme's creation was a far cry from designing and implementing a grand blueprint. In fact, it was developed as an *ad hoc* instrument to bring some flexibility into a system where the allowed level of total emissions had already been fixed by existing performance standards.[19] Confronted with the problem that existing legislation blocked the location of new activities and even the growth of existing firms, the authorities had to do something to reduce the burden of this self-imposed scarcity by allowing specific forms of exchange.

The market which consequently evolved carried with it the rudiments of its earlier stage which largely explains why the number of trades (and, hence, economic efficiency) was low, albeit that the much needed flexibility was introduced into the system and environmental integrity was largely maintained.

The failure to achieve economic efficiency is often attributed by the literature to the following market imperfections:

(a) regulatory restrictions on trade;

(b) uncertainty over the status of property rights;

(c) high transaction costs.

Uncertainty as to the status of the property rights limited trading. Uncertainty as to whether the sellers would achieve their reductions (buyer's liability) on the buyer's baseline and whether trades would be accepted further inhibited full scale trading.

Part of this arose from the conflicting interests of environmentalists and businesses which led to the creation of policies with no explicit definition of the nature of the property right in question. Distrust in emissions trading arises, in part, from the generally held view that property rights, once assigned, are immutable and, so, could allow unrestrained use of the property in question.

In summary, the market imperfections that impaired the cost-effectiveness of the earlier US Emissions Trading Programmes were largely a consequence of crafting a market onto an existing system of direct regulation in the form of emission standards. These 'rules' for increasing flexibility were more a compliment to, than a substitute for, existing emissions policies.

---

19 Klaassen, G and Nentjes, A, 'Sulfur trading under the 1990 CAAA in the US: an assessment of first experiences' (1997) 153 Journal of Institutional and Theoretical Economics 384.

LESSONS LEARNT AND APPLIED:
THE SO$_2$ ACID RAIN PROGRAMME

As stated above, in 1990, the Clean Air Act Amendment became law in the USA. Title IV of these amendments contains provisions to provide for the control of acid deposition caused by sulphur and nitrogen oxide emissions. The SO$_2$ ARP introduced a nationwide emissions trading scheme for electricity producers.

In contrast with the EPA's earlier Emissions Trading Programme, the SO$_2$ ARP was designed with the twofold objective of reducing drastically the SO$_2$ emissions of the electricity sector and to provide from the start an institutional framework for a genuine market in emissions allowances with minimum regulatory restrictions or other market interference by the authorities.[20] The basic structure of the SO$_2$ ARP can be listed as follows:

(a) emissions allowances and authorisation to emit one ton of SO$_2$ during or after a specific year;

(b) allowances made available equal to the level of allowed emissions;

(c) allocation of allowances is based on a system of free distribution amongst firms in proportion to their average fuel consumption in the period 1985–87 ('grandfathering');

(d) flexibility to emit more or less than the allocation provided through the option to sell, buy or bank allowances;

(e) government withholds 2.8% of annual allowances for auction and directs sale in case liquidity of market is low;

(f) compliance is determined at the end of the year. Units are granted a further 30 days, during which allowances may be purchased to cover emissions;

(g) if a facility's emissions exceed the number of allowances held, a statutory penalty of US$2,500 (previously US$2,000) is automatically imposed for each ton of SO$_2$ by which a facility exceeds the allowances held.

No special institutional framework was laid down for the creation of a secondary market in which allowances could be traded. It is widely suggested in the literature that there was no need, since the general rules of the SO$_2$ ARP are such as to provide for such a market, as has proven to be the case. For example, in 1996 over 4 m tons worth of SO$_2$ allowances were transferred between unrelated parties. Some of the specific aspects of the design of the SO$_2$ ARP often cited[21] for this success are:

---

20 See *op cit*, Boyle, fn 15.
21 See www.unfccc.de; http://cop6.unfccc.int; and see *op cit*, Boyle, fn 15.

(a) clear specification of initial allowances per annum for a 30 year period;

(b) by defining allowances as the permission to emit one tonne of SO_2 during or after a specific year, the traded commodity was considerably more homogenous;

(c) transactions facilitated by the possibility to trade emissions allowances on a 1:1 basis;

(d) absence of regulatory approval procedures reduces administration costs, eliminates sources of uncertainty and contributes in both ways to the lowering of transaction costs;

(e) absence of restrictions in participation allowances can be bought by any person, not only utility representatives, but also private companies, brokers, municipalities, environment groups, etc.

It is widely believed that the expansion of the market and homogenisation of the 'commodity' that is traded has reduced transactional costs enormously. As a result, brokerage fees are often around 5% compared with brokerage fees of up to 30% under the EPA Emissions Trading Programme.[22]

WHAT IS THE NATURE OF THE ALLOWANCES: ARE THEY PROPERTY?

If a failure to characterise property rights is likely to hinder the efficient operation of an emissions trading system, what are the legal or other criteria that need to be specified to give the markets the certainty on this issue they seem to require?

The word 'property' is not a term of art, but takes its meaning from its context. Decided legal cases, it would seem, can only provide an indication of the characteristics of 'property' in the context of pseudo property like permits.[23] The Court of Appeal, in *Celtic Extraction Ltd and Bluestone Chemicals v The Environment Agency*,[24] was called upon to consider whether or not a waste management licence was property for the purposes of s 436 of the Insolvency Act 1986. The court developed three tests which it considered needed to be satisfied before such a permit could be considered to be property:

---

22 See *op cit*, Boyle, fn 15.
23 *Celtic Extraction Ltd and Bluestone Chemicals v the Environment Agency* [2000] 2 WLR 991.
24 *Ibid*.

(a) there must be a statutory framework conferring entitlement on one who satisfies certain conditions, even though there is some element of discretion exercisable within the framework;

(b) the permit must be transferable;

(c) the exemption or licence will have value.

The court relied on a number of previous UK and overseas decisions. In particular, the case of the *Commonwealth of Australia v WMC Resources Ltd*,[25] in which the court was called upon to decide whether or not a permit to explore for petroleum in an area of the continental shelf granted under the Petroleum (Submerged Lands) Act 1987 was property within the meaning of the Petroleum (Australia-Indonesia Zone of Co-operation) (Consequential Provisions) Act 1990 which required the Commonwealth to provide 'just terms' for any acquisition of property. The court cited with approval the test applied by the court as below:

> ... the rights ... were clearly identifiable, assignable, stable, potentially a very substantial value, and not, because of their statutory foundation feasible.

These decisions and others, particularly, of the European Court of Human Rights[26] in relation to whether or not licences or permits are possessions protected by Art 1 of Protocol 1 of the European Convention of Human Rights,[27] and various academic articles addressing the question of whether tradeable emissions allowances would constitute property protected by the Takings Clause of the US Constitution,[28] give us some idea of what characteristics the courts are likely to require emissions allowances to possess before they would hold them to be property.

However, perhaps it is these characteristics themselves that are more important in providing for a functioning and liquid market in emissions allowances, rather than whether or not such allowances are to be called property or not.

It is clear that the SO_2 allowances created under the US SO_2 ARP have a majority of these characteristics, but that s 765(1)(b) of Title IV to the US Clean Air Act 1990 states quite categorically that the allowances allocated under the SO_2 ARP do not constitute property rights. The success in the SO_2 ARP market would seem to suggest that it does not matter whether or not the

---

25 (1998) 152 ALR 1.

26 *Pine Valley Developments Ltd and Others v Ireland* (No1) (1991) 14 EHRR 319.

27 Smyth, M, *Business and the Human Rights Act 1998*, 2000, Bristol: Jordans, pp 326–30.

28 Leach, P, *Taking a Case to the European Court of Human Rights*, 2001, London: Blackstone; Austin, SA, 'Comment, tradeable emissions programs: implications under the [US] Takings Clause' (1996) 26 Env Liability 323; and Savage, J, 'Confiscation of emission reduction credits: the case for compensation under the Takings Clause (1997) 16 Va Env E1 LJ (Winter) 227.

allowances are property *per se*. What does matter is that such allowances have many of the characteristics of property and, more particularly, of harmogenised commodities, for example, they are interchangeable, it is clear who has rights to them, there are no regulatory restrictions on trading and, finally, no major restrictions on participation in the market.

UK'S EMISSIONS TRADING FRAMEWORK

The proposed ETS has to some extent been designed by a business-led initiative, the UK Emissions Trading Group (ETG), set up jointly by the Confederation of British Industry and the Advisory Committee on Business and the Environment.[29]

The Framework Document confirms that the ETS will cover either carbon dioxide (CO_2) emissions only or CO_2 plus the other five GHGs (that is, methane, nitrous oxide, hydrofluorocarbons, perfluorocarbons and sulphur hexafluoride). To begin with, there will be two major, but mutually exclusive, ways to obtain access to the ETS: (i) voluntary participation as described above (Direct Entry Participants); and (ii) as a party to a Climate Change Levy Agreement (CCLA).

The eligibility criteria discussed below make it clear that the ETS is aimed at energy users, rather than energy generators or suppliers, that is, it is a 'downstream' scheme. It is made clear that, in the short term, there is no direct role for electricity generators in the ETS, other than perhaps the supply of credits into the ETS from approved emissions reduction projects.

Entry to the ETS is initially to be on a voluntary basis only. The bidding process of March 2002 took the form of a 'descending clock' auction continuing until the total prices bid, multiplied by the quantity of tonnes of CO_2 reductions bid, is less than or equal to £215 m. At this point, all live bids become binding. For each successful bidder, the single quantity of emissions reductions bid will be divided into five absolute emissions caps over the period 2002–06.

The timetable set out in the Framework Document is for the ETS to run with effect from 1 April 2002, later than originally anticipated. From this time, successful Direct Entry Participants hold allowances permitting the holder to emit a given quantity of CO_2 or its equivalent.

Direct Entry Participants will, subject to the rules of the ETS, be totally free to trade these allowances – an approach often referred to as 'cap and trade'. On 31 December 2002, the first compliance period ends. There will then be a reconciliation period from 1 January until 31 March 2003 for Direct Entry

---

29 ETG Proposals to Government for a UK ETS, March 2000 (www.etg.com).

Participants' emissions to be verified and reported to the Emissions Trading Authority (ETA) and, if necessary, to carry out any trading to ensure they hold enough allowances to cover their actual emissions during that compliance period. Incentive payments equal to one-fifth of the total incentive awarded will be made in April 2003 to those who hold a sufficient number of allowances at the end of the reconciliation period. This process will be repeatedly annually.

DIRECT ENTRY ELIGIBILITY CRITERIA

The Framework Document states that 'any person with sufficient legal capacity to enter into a binding contract who is carrying out activities in the UK which give rise to either direct or indirect GHG emissions is eligible for entry into the scheme'. Therefore, an entity would need to be recognised under UK law as having legal personality.

Where an entity is eligible to enter the ETS, not all sources operated by it may be included. For example, those sources which generate energy on-site for use off-site, that is, the electricity generators, will not be eligible. Neither will sources covered by a CCLA, nor those over which the Direct Entry Participant does not have management control, for example, some joint venture arrangements.

CLIMATE CHANGE LEVY NEGOTIATED AGREEMENTS

Since 1 April 2001, the CCL of £0.43/kwh for electricity and £0.15/kwh for gas and coal has been payable on all business use of electricity, gas and coal. This is to be collected by the utility companies as part of customers' energy bills. Only the transport sector and domestic sectors will be exempt. This 'downstream energy tax'[30] is being applied to all energy used, whether or not such energy is derived from fossil fuel (that is, it is not a carbon tax). However, those considered to be heavy users of energy (defined by reference to the Integrated Pollution Prevention and Control Directive)[31] are eligible for an 80% discount from the CCL if they have entered into CCLAs with the

---

30 Finance Act 2000, s 30 and Scheds 6 and 7.
31 Council Directive 96/61/EC, OJ L 257/26, 10.10.96; this approach is used because it was not possible to develop a workable definition of a heavy user. Note that the limitations and thresholds in those A1 and A2 process descriptions do not apply for the purpose of eligibility.

government, thereby having taken on emissions or energy targets linked to tonnes of CO_2 emitted. Unlike the Direct Entry Participants, CCLA Participants will have either an absolute target (linked to absolute emissions of CO_2) or a relative target (linked to emissions of CO_2 relative to output).

The important point for this discussion is that the parties to the CCLAs are to be permitted to trade allowances to meet their targets. However, they will only be able to obtain allowances to sell when they have demonstrated performance above their targets; this approach is referred to in the Framework Document as 'baseline and credit'. In effect, CCLA Participants will only be issued allowances after each of the two year compliance dates, for example, 1 April 2003, 1 April 2005, etc. In fact, CCLA Participants have no targets for the non-milestone years in between and, so, cannot generate allowances in those years.

The Framework Document makes it clear that those in the relative (rather than the absolute) sector will have certain restrictions placed on their freedom to trade allowances so as to reduce the potential for allowance 'inflation'. The major restriction proposed is a 'gateway' which would work on a 'one in, one out' basis between the ETS and the relative sector. The gateway would only permit allowances from the relative sector into the ETS to the extent that the same number of allowances have previously moved in the opposite direction.

It is also proposed that, while voluntary participants and those with absolute targets under the CCLAs will be able to bank allowances into future commitment periods and to buy allowances from international and domestic emissions reduction projects, those with relative targets will not.

GOVERNANCE

To begin with, there will be a pseudo ETA which will sit within central government. The Framework Document expressly states that, in the longer term, the ETA will be established as a statutory independent body, although no date is given for when this is likely to happen.

Whatever the legal status of the ETA, its main function will be to record the holdings of any transfer of allowances between participants and enforce compliance. It is envisaged that trades will take place in real time electronically through secure internet links. Whilst the government is not proposing to publish price details of individual transactions, it is proposing collecting this information and publishing it in an aggregated form.

ALLOWANCES AND TRADING

The tradeable units within the ETS will be emissions reduction 'allowances'. Allowances will be created by government, unless imported from recognised international sources. These allowances, as provided for under the Kyoto Protocol, will be denominated in tonnes of CO_2 or its equivalent and each will have a unique serial number. For the non-CO_2 GHGs an index allows a comparison against the equivalent in global warming impact of a tonne of CO2, hence the reference to CO_2 or its equivalent.

When Direct Entry Participants receive their allocation of allowances on 1 April 2002 and, thereafter, on 1 January of each year, these will be held in the Participants' compliance accounts. CCLA Participants who wish to trade will need to have a separate Compliance Account for each facility, subject to a CCLA that proposes to trade.

There will be four distinct types of account within the ETA: compliance accounts; trading accounts; a national retirement account; and national cancellation accounts.

It will be necessary for all participants to open a trading account to facilitate actual trading and non-participants will be free to open trading accounts. This will be of interest to traders, brokers, Non-Government Organisations and, perhaps, even overseas companies which might want to purchase UK allowances on the basis that they are likely to be recognised and count towards targets imposed in their own country at some future date.

Trading and compliance accounts will be designated as either relative or absolute sector accounts. There will be no restrictions on transfers between trading accounts in the same sector, or for transfers from an absolute to a relative trading account. However, transfers from a relative to an absolute trading account will be subject to the gateway controls described earlier.

The national retirement account will hold all allowances which have been used by participants against their emissions target with the effect of cancelling allowances, whilst the cancellation account allows for the voluntary cancellation of allowances.

It is important to understand that the registry will not function as an exchange. The commercial transactions themselves, whether they be simple bilateral trades or more complicated ones, utilising brokers or even derivative markets, will take place elsewhere. However, as mentioned above, brokers and others may open trading accounts, which should help to facilitate a more sophisticated market. Once a commercial trade has been completed, the seller will make the transfer using a secure website link in much the same way that one would use online banking. Such transfers will be final, with the possible exception of transfer of relative allowances through the gateway to the absolute sector. If the gateway is closed, the transfer will not be completed. It is not clear whether the transfer will fail altogether or whether it will be put into a queue until such time as the gateway is again open.

SOME TECHNICAL ISSUES

If targets are to represent real reductions in emissions it will be necessary to establish a business' actual emissions over a given period (its 'baseline'). Once this has been done, a target can be set for future emissions which represents, if achieved, real emissions reductions.

The Framework Document proposes that, for entrants to the ETS in 2001, the baseline should be average annual emissions for the three years up to and including 2000. However, entrants may be allowed to use a shorter period if they can satisfy external verifiers (see below) that they do not have access to sufficient information for all three years. One likely issue of equal concern to initial entrants and those who enter at a later date is that the earlier Consultation Paper did not indicate how baselines will be calculated for future entrants into the current ETS. It simply stated, unhelpfully, that the baseline for future entrants shall be decided at some future time. The only guidance given was that 'any decision will be governed by the principle that early entrants should not be penalised for their early commitment to the ETS': this principle is often referred to as 'baseline protection'. It seems that government has suggested in some quarters that, if there is to be a mandatory scheme in future, then the baseline under such a mandatory scheme will not be based on a period later than 2000–01, so providing some level of baseline protection to current participants. The later Framework Document does not provide the hope for detail either.

As the ETS is to be applied to energy users rather than energy producers (a downstream scheme), it will cover both direct and indirect emissions. Targets will be based on CO_2 emissions only or, subject to their being verifiable, on all six GHGs actually emitted. It is thought that if participants were able to choose between the GHGs they would 'cherry pick' the easiest to reduce, ignoring the others. Electricity used by an entity will constitute an indirect emission for which conversion factors have been developed to convert the amount of electricity used into CO_2 equivalent emissions.

Whatever the energy usage by an entity, be it direct, indirect or a mixture of both, reliable and verifiable protocols are needed for monitoring these emissions, so that entities can provide reliable reports on obligated GHG emissions. Protocols for CO_2 emissions have now been developed. These will, where practicable, also be used for the CCLAs so as to minimise administrative burdens on participants. Similar protocols for the other five GHGs are being developed for some processes. However, those potential participants expressing an interest to join the ETS, but who wish to include

GHGs for processes for which protocols have not been developed, were required to make this known to the government by the end of July 2001. The onus will be on these participants to develop suitable protocols and have these approved by the government.

If the ETS is to be credible and deliver the real emissions reductions needed to meet the UK's national emissions reduction targets, robust verification of the emissions data reported by participants will be essential. The proposed method for achieving this is through external accredited verifiers. There would then be fuller checks carried out periodically. Such fuller checks would presumably be made by the ETA, but this is not made clear. This approach largely follows that used to verify the performance of those companies which have joined externally verified environmental management systems, such as ISO 14001. Those companies wishing to offer verification services will need to be appropriately certified. Discussions are under way with the United Kingdom Accreditation Service to determine how this will be done.

ENFORCEMENT

Trading will operate on the basis of 'seller liability' so that allowances remain valid irrespective of the compliance status of the seller. Therefore, buyers can be certain that what they are buying has value without the need to carry out due diligence, which could drive up transaction costs. If the environmental integrity of the system is to be preserved, against freeriders generating allowances without real reductions, there needs to be an effective system of enforcement.

In the US sulphur dioxide trading system, set up under the 1990 Amendment to the Clean Air Act, a statutory fine of US$2,500 is imposed for every tonne of SO_2 by which a facility in breach has missed its target. Considering that, in that market, a tonne of SO_2 could trade for as low as US$100, the penalty is in financial terms quite draconian, but according to the literature effective.

Of course, there are some fundamental differences between that system and the proposed ETS. The US SO_2 trading program is based on legislation; it is a fairly homogeneous upstream scheme in that it applies to power stations only and it is mandatory. The ETS is to use existing administrative powers, it is a downstream system open to a wide range of industry sectors, and it is to be voluntary. These differences make the task of setting up effective enforcement mechanisms for the ETS a difficult one.

Initially, there will be no express statutory sanctions for breaches of the rules; but government proposes that the ETS be brought into force in two stages. In the first stage, the enforcement mechanisms are to consist of nonpayment of the financial incentive in any one year and, if at the end of the five years the total target is missed, clawback of all incentive payments made. In addition, Direct Entry Participants that fail to meet their annual target could have their following year's allocations of allowances reduced by the amount their emissions exceeded target. Persistent offenders may also face being 'named and shamed' and even expelled from the ETS. It is also suggested in the Framework Document that reliance could be placed on general criminal law. There are some doubts over how effective this is likely to be in practice.

The other suggestion made is that the Direct Entry Participants might themselves agree to a self-imposed regime of penalties for breaches of the ETS rules. Such a regime would most likely have to rely on some form of contractual arrangement between the Participants. Case law suggests that there may be some problems in relying on contractual penalties. However, it is possible that the courts may take a more enlightened view about the use of contractual penalties to underwrite schemes such as this.

It is presumed that the statement in the Framework Document that the government intends to create a statutory offence as soon as is practicable is the implied second stage.

OTHER SOURCES OF ALLOWANCES OR CREDITS

In time, other domestic schemes could generate tradable 'credits' capable of being traded into the ETS: for example Green Certificates (Renewables Obligation Certificates – ROCs) relating to the renewable energy obligation of electricity suppliers, credits for energy efficiency projects in business, other than those in the main trading schemes and domestic emissions reduction projects. The fact that the government currently does not propose recognising credits from international projects such as the clean development mechanism (CDM) and joint initiatives (JI) provided for under the Kyoto Protocol until the rules for these mechanisms are settled in the international negotiations is seen by some as a mistake. Allowances from some overseas emissions trading schemes may also be recognised by the ETS before their recognition under the Kyoto Protocol commitment period which should begin in 2008. There is, however, a question mark over what value pre-2008 allowances will have after 2008. The current proposal is that all allowances and credits (other than allowances from the relative sector) may be banked for use in future years, until 2007, followed by a percentage limit on the number of allowances which can be carried over into the Kyoto commitment period (2008–12). The government promises to announce the exact form of any such restriction at least three years before 2008.

UK-BASED EMISSIONS REDUCTION PROJECTS

Whilst the government is proposing to delay a final decision on whether or not to accept credits from JI and CDMs into the UK ETS, it does intend to press ahead with approval of UK based emissions reduction projects. It is hoped that such projects will encourage emissions reductions in areas not covered by the ETS or CCLAs, for example, transport, household energy efficiency and businesses not covered by either the ETS or CCLAs.

The rules that govern such domestic projects have yet to be finalised but are likely to follow closely the rules for JI projects. The main requirement will be that such projects will need to demonstrate that any proposed emissions reductions will be additional to a 'business as usual' baseline. In essence, this means that the project would not have been undertaken as a part of the company's normal development or expansion, but has been implemented solely or largely for the purpose of achieving emissions reductions. It is also envisaged that such projects will be subject to monitoring and verification procedures to at least the same standards as overseas JI and CDM projects will be.

The Framework Document considers it unlikely that all the necessary detail and rules for project approval will be in place for the beginning of the ETS. However, it does state that the government is considering drawing up an interim list of projects with pre-agreed baselines that can be approved before all the necessary rules and approvals have been finalised, so that a number of such projects can be authorised and begun. Such projects may include some renewable energy technologies, but will almost certainly exclude carbon sequestration projects such as forestry initiatives.

INTERNATIONAL TRADING[32]

The Kyoto Protocol, an international treaty, provides for trading between sovereign States. Businesses or companies will, however, only have access to trading within a nation State if that State's domestic law provides for it. Further, if two companies each resident in a different Annex 1 State wish to trade with each other, domestic law in each State will need to recognise the allowances of the other State. If it does not, there is not necessarily an absolute prohibition on such trading, but the price of any allowances traded is likely to be heavily discounted to take into account the risk that such allowances may not subsequently be recognised and, therefore, usable, in the emissions trading scheme under which the buyer is obligated. There are already

---

32   Hobley, A, 'Emissions trading in the UK: an overview' (2001) 1 Env Liability 3.

examples of such speculative trading having taken place, albeit the price per tonne of CO_2 has been as low as $1.

CONCLUSION

One could take the view that the ETS is a pilot programme[33] to allow UK business and government to 'learn by doing', so making the UK a centre of expertise in this new market, in which case it is a reasonable assumption that the ETS will achieve this objective. It is, therefore, not expected that it will be perfect. In fact, there is time before 2008 to make mistakes and to learn from them. On this basis, the ETS will probably work in the short term, as some companies perceive commercial first mover advantages.

Perhaps the biggest question is whether there will emerge a healthy and efficient market in the trading of emissions allowances. The proposed ETS seems to incorporate many lessons learnt from the US SO_2 trading program. These include seller liability; not requiring regulatory approval of transfers; basing the scheme, to some degree, on a single, interchangeable emissions unit; and providing for a registry which will allow absolute transparency of who holds the rights in the allowances. However, there are some worries. There is some concern over how effective the proposed penalties will be and if ineffective penalties could lead to 'free riders' generating cheap allowances without achieving real emissions reductions. Second, could the restrictions on relative sector allowances prove too restrictive, so driving up transaction costs, and possibly reducing market liquidity?

Inherent in the government's 'learn by doing' approach is the risk of putting in place systems that may turn out to be incompatible with those developed internationally. The government clearly expects economic advantages for the UK, its businesses and the City of London which it believes will be well placed to play a leading and influential role in the development of such schemes internationally. Business would seem to share this view, since the form of the proposed ETS owes much to the initiatives of business itself.

---

33 Marshall, Lord, 'Economic instruments and the business use of energy', Report submitted to the UK Government, 1998.

CHAPTER 8

US V UK APPROACHES TO ENVIRONMENTAL RISK

Michael Quint[1]

INTRODUCTION

This paper considers some of the differences that exist between United States and United Kingdom approaches to environmental risk. The focus is on identifying differences in Quantitative Risk Assessment (QRA) methodology, since this is where the author has most experience. Possible underlying social and political reasons are also identified, along with the implications of these differences for international environmental policy development.

QUANTITATIVE RISK ASSESSMENT

QRA has been used as a key part of environmental management in the USA for over 20 years. Originating from the regulatory toxicology practices of food and drug safety, it relies on combining simulations of environmental exposure with quantitative dose-response estimates generated from toxicological studies, to give numerical estimates of risk, in the form of an 'increased lifetime risks of cancer' or 'hazard index' levels.[2] The exposure simulations require chemical transport modelling, along with assumptions concerning human behaviour, while dose-response estimates are derived from laboratory tests on animals or human epidemiology studies.

From its early beginnings in which the focus was on single chemicals[3] and single exposure pathways[4] QRA has developed to enable multi-pathway and multi-chemical exposure scenarios to be modelled. This has made it applicable to many environmental situations, such as contaminated land and incinerators, where it involves the use of complex multi-pathway mathematical modelling techniques. These techniques include advanced

---

1   Michael Quint is a technical director at Parsons Brinckerhoff. Michael was educated at Oxford University and he has over 12 years' experience of assessing environmental risks and liabilities. He has also helped to develop government guidance in this area. He can be contacted by email: QuintM@pbworld.com.
2   Ratios of modelled doses to safe doses.
3   Eg, lead.
4   Eg, drinking water.

methods, such as Monte Carlo sampling, and they typically necessitate the use of a computer.

While QRA is the dominant decision making tool in the US, its use in the UK is not widespread. This is in spite of the UK government's stated objective of using it more widely, as described in the Department of the Environment, Transport and the Regions (DETR) document entitled *Guidelines for Environmental Risk Assessment and Management*.[5]

Brief summaries of key aspects of the US and UK approaches to QRA are provided below. Reference is made to contaminated land risk assessment methodology, as this is an important area for the application of risk based approaches, and it provides examples of specific differences in methodology.

US APPROACHES

Environmental QRA in the US is characterised by the following:

(a) well resourced;[6]

(b) extensive government support and guidance;

(c) large number of practitioners;

(d) high level of technical competency in regulatory community;

(e) focus on human health.

In terms of specific observations relating to contaminated land, it is common practice in the US to:

(a) perform quantitative site specific risk assessments on most sites;

(b) assume an on-site drinking water well exists or may exist on every site;

(c) assume an on-site residential scenario;

(d) use exposure factors[7] prescribed by central (EPA) or State governments;

(e) use dose-response estimates prescribed by central or State governments;

(f) use low dose extrapolation techniques to assess cancer risk;

(g) assume that B2 carcinogens (animal evidence only) are carcinogenic to humans;

(h) ignore background intakes of non-carcinogens;

(i) use approaches, which are in line with Superfund guidance;

(j) perform uncertainty analysis and Monte Carlo simulations.

---

5   2000, London: DETR.

6   Eg, can cost upwards of £30,000 for a site specific assessment.

7   Eg, soil ingestion rates.

UK APPROACHES

Environmental QRA in the UK is characterised by the following:

(a) relatively poorly resourced;[8]

(b) limited government support and guidance, except for general policy statements;

(c) limited number of practitioners;

(d) low level of technical competency in regulatory community;

(e) focus on broad environmental issues, including human health.

In terms of specific requirements for conducting contaminated land risk assessments, it is common practice in the UK to:

(a) avoid quantitative risk assessment, if possible;

(b) use generic soil quality standards in assessments of risk;

(c) ignore potential land use and focus solely on current land use;

(d) not assume an on-site well exists when one is not present;

(e) use *ad hoc* exposure factors[9] chosen from various sources;

(f) use dose-response estimates from the World Health Organisation and overseas (including the Environmental Protection Agency).

Further requirements for UK contaminated land risk assessment are apparent from draft Environment Agency and DETR guidance documents, which suggest that:

(a) low dose extrapolation must not be used when assessing risk from carcinogens;

(b) B2 (animal evidence only) carcinogens must not be treated as human carcinogens;

(c) background intakes must be addressed when assessing non-carcinogenic risk;

(d) synergistic effects must be addressed;

(e) the Contaminated Land Exposure Assessment model should be used in most cases.

---

8   Rarely costs exceed £10,000 for a site specific risk assessment.
9   Eg, soil ingestion rates.

DIFFERENCES BETWEEN THE APPROACHES

A review of the above suggests that there are several key differences between risk assessment approaches in the two countries, as follows:

(a) US risk assessments tend to focus more on human health than UK;

(b) the UK has embraced risk assessment less enthusiastically than the US, to date;

(c) there appears to be much less guidance and expertise in the UK than in the US;

(d) approaches to dose-response estimation differ in the two countries;

(e) approaches to exposure assessment differ in the two countries.

The first of these differences may be explained by the fact that human health issues have attracted wider support in the US, when raised by environmental activists, than have conservation issues. This may be because of the greater sense of individual freedoms and rights that exists in US society, as indicated by the deeply embedded right to the pursuit of 'life, liberty and happiness'. Health risks from environmental sources are clearly an unwelcome infringement of such a basic right and, indeed, this was a cornerstone of early court challenges to the concept of 'insignificant risk'.

Other factors influencing the dominance of health issues in the US include a legacy of Nixon's 'war on cancer' in the 1970s and the influence of well publicised examples of ill-health resulting from pollution.[10] More recently, even Hollywood has been getting in on the act.[11]

The second and third of the differences could be explained by the UK's historic scepticism towards science and a lack of trained graduates in the required fields of chemistry, mathematics and, especially, toxicology. Various forces conspire to make the UK seem like an anti-scientific society at times, not least of which are the recent examples of science seeming to act against the public interest, such as BSE.

Further resistance to the use of risk based methods in the UK may stem from them being seen as redundant in the face of widespread acceptance of the precautionary principle. This is an overly simplistic view, however, since instead of representing alternative approaches to addressing environmental risk, they can be used together, with the precautionary principle being invoked in the making of assumptions within a QRA, whenever knowledge or data are lacking.

---

10 Eg, Love Canal, see Levine, A, *Love Canal: Science, Politics and People*, 1982, New York: Lexington; and Times Beach, see Reko, HK, *Not an Act of God: The Story of Times Beach*, 1984, St Louis: Lindell.

11 Eg, *Erin Brockovich, Civil Action.*

Another reason for the limited role of QRA in the UK may be the recent report from the Royal Commission on Environmental Pollution, which stated that environmental standards should be set on the basis of both science and public opinion. Again, this seems to downgrade science's role in providing answers to environmental questions. This can be contrasted with the US where there seems to be a greater respect for science. In fact, the US 'can do' attitude can be said to extend to science, whereby ignorance is regarded as a temporary obstacle on the way to knowledge, and it can be removed with enough research time and money.

Importantly, regulatory and civil penalties for causing harm to human health or the environment are much lower in the UK than they are in the US. The UK lacks a system of punitive damages and contract law still underpins dealings with the public. This can be contrasted with the strength of consumer legislation in the US, especially the ability to mount class actions, the size of damage awards and the willingness to look beyond the contract. Clearly, and as a result, there is a financial imperative to assessing and minimising environmental risk to humans, which is perhaps lacking in the UK.

In regard to the specific differences in approach, dose-response estimation is a subjective process and there are key differences of opinion between US and UK government officials charged with setting health based standards. This applies particularly to carcinogens. On the exposure assessment side, UK planning legislation allows greater control over land use, hence the worst case scenario of residential development (from a site sensitivity point of view) can be controlled by legal instruments.[12]

While the above may seem rather negative towards the UK, there are positive sides to our more measured use of QRA. For example, we tend to take a more pragmatic approach in its application, avoiding complex risk based simulations when there does not appear to be any clear benefit in doing so. This is in contrast to the US, where extensive QRA has often been carried out when the solution to the problem is already known.

WHAT THESE DIFFERENCES MEAN IN PRACTICE

The differences identified above are important considerations for reviewers of risk assessments in the US and UK and they provide a guide as to how QRA may develop here as an environmental decision making tool. In addition, they give clues to wider issues relating to the two countries, such as how environmental matters are viewed and dealt with politically. For example, the

---

12 Similarly, the wide availability of mains water in our much smaller country, plus controls over abstraction exercised by the Environment Agency, mean that the worst case scenario of an on-site drinking water well can often be avoided.

current differences of opinion over Kyoto may be explicable as a conflict between the relative weightings each country places on science and the precautionary principle. If this is the case, then we can expect further disputes, especially as under World Trade Organisation (WTO) rules any impediment to free trade on health or environmental grounds must be 'scientifically based'.

CONCLUSION

In conclusion, while QRA is used for environmental decision making in both the US and UK, differences exist between how widely it is applied and the approaches taken. These differences may be explained by underlying socio-political issues, differences of scientific opinion and the respective regulatory settings. The differences give clues to wider issues relating to the two countries, and may shed light on the current Kyoto disagreement. In the opinion of the author, such disagreements are likely to become more common, as WTO requirements take effect.

CHAPTER 9

(PRE)CAUTIONARY TALES: RISK, REGULATION AND THE PRECAUTIONARY PRINCIPLE

Robert Lee[1]

Physicians of the utmost fame

Were called at once; but when they came

They answered, as they took their fees,

'There is no cure for this disease'

Hilaire Belloc

Cautionary Tales: Henry King (who died as a result of his diet of string)

RISK SOCIETY

One of the most influential social science texts of the last decade of the 20th century was unquestionably Beck's book on risk society.[2] The thesis concerns a move away from industrial society with its concern with the distribution of wealth towards a risk society in which there is an increasing focus on the costs of development, or, as Lash and Wynne would have it, a shift from the distribution of goods to the distribution of 'bads'.[3] Giddens[4] has pointed out that the bads or risks are not simply dangers, but constitute uncertainties, especially concerning the impact of developments in science and technology. This uncertainty is heightened as, unlike the costs attaching to industrial society, those borne in risk society are spread in a random and differential manner. This has had major consequences for the political system, as debate moves from the relations of production to the production of ill-defined relations with risk. In Beck's own words, 'what no one saw and no one wanted – self-endangerment and devastation of nature – is becoming a major force of history'.[5]

---

1 Robert Lee is Professor of Law and the former head of Cardiff Law School. At present he is a co-director of the Economic and Social Research Council Centre for Business Relationships, Accountability, Sustainability and Society, Cardiff Law School, editor of *Environment Law Monthly* and environmental editor of the *Journal of Business Law*, a member of the training committee of the Law Society of England and Wales and of the Lord Chancellor's Standing Committee on Legal Education. He can be contacted by email: LeeRG@cardiff.ac.uk.

2 Beck, U, *Risk Society: Towards a New Modernity*, 1992, London: Sage.

3 *Ibid*, Lash, S and Wynne, B, in their introduction to the English language text of Beck.

4 Giddens, A, 'Risk and responsibility' (1999) 62 MLR 1.

5 Beck, U, *Ecological Enlightenment*, 1995, Cambridge: Polity.

If Beck is right, then one way of viewing events such as the demonstrations in Seattle might be a rejection of the costs attaching to techno-economic growth – a point at which a fear of the downsides of the price that *may* attach to such 'progress' outweighs any value placed on further development. This emphasis on risk grows out of its intangible, uncertain, and unpredictable quality. People may know that they do not understand all of the issues; they may know that, ultimately, there may be no hazard attaching to that that which they fear. But this causes greater not lesser debate, as they thirst for knowledge to help define the risk. As Giddens explains, there is a pre-occupation with the future and with a world that 'we are both exploring and seeking to normalise and control' as we live on 'a high technological frontier which absolutely no one completely understands and which generates a diversity of possible futures'.[6]

This leads us to Beck's sub-title and indeed his sub-text, 'reflexive modernisation'. By this Beck refers to individualised responses as we learn to cope with the risks of modernisation. Reflexive modernisation describes the feeling of a way ahead in the dark shadow of progress. It represents a different sort of progress as society turns back in on modernity, seeking to adjust or redefine its regulatory enterprise. This reflexivity encompassing as it does our continual re-evaluation of the goals of modernisation is found in individual responses to everyday choices (such as whether to buy genetically modified (GM) foods), but such responses can be collectively identified, understood and labelled. 'Reflexive modernisation' is distrustful of science. It is often resentful of scientific endeavour, not least because society sees itself as the subject of experimentation. Elsewhere, I have argued[7] that, ironically, in seeking to control nature, the boundaries between the natural world have become blurred to the point of confusion. Others might describe this as the death of nature, by which they mean that nature has been strangled by human hands.

Reflexive modernisation has changed our view of and relationships with science and scientists. We begin to understand science as something other than a value neutral enterprise, and certainly not as a unitary body of knowledge, even though some views may be presented as mainstream. Although this doubting of scientific rationality might seem a straightforward matter, it has been learnt by hard lessons. Thus, having been assured by experts that BSE prions could not cross a hypothesised species barrier, we cannot yet forecast the extent of new variant CJD in human beings.[8] It

---

6   See *op cit*, Giddens, fn 4, p 3.
7   Along with Derek Morgan – see Lee, R and Morgan, D, *Human Fertilisation and Embryology, Regulating the Reproductive Revolution*, 2001, London: Blackstone.
8   Cousens, SN *et al*, 'Predicting the CJD epidemic in humans' nature' (1997) 385 Nature 197; Meikle, J, 'Millions at risk from CJD say EU experts' (2000) *The Guardian*, 8 January.

transpires that the Southwood BSE working party worried about the risk of transfer of BSE to humans via vaccines, but that this risk was described in the final report of the group as 'remote'. The Department of Health had not wished to start a scare about pharmaceutical products given that certain vaccines came from bovine serum.[9] Ironically, it seems that the pet food industry eventually had more success in procuring a ban on bovine offal.

This sort of episode has led to the common use of labels such as 'government scientists', set implicitly against other scientific views from NGOs or elsewhere in debates that have transferred from the laboratory to the television studio – or, indeed, the internet. It has helped shift issues of risk to the heart of politics, creating distrust and disenchantment with politicians seen as wedded to the interests of modernisation. Curiously, Beck, writing in the 1980s, foresaw the growth of risk conflicts and growing protestation against science.[10] There is much literature from the scientific community that is resentful of the opening up of debate in this way,[11] but while government is slow to learn the lesson, this must be seen as an encouraging development. It is only by participation in the debate that the uncertainties of risk society can be addressed – which leads us, at last, to the precautionary principle.

In this context, the precautionary principle assumes some importance for, in asserting the rationality of prudence in the face of risk, those advocating the application of the principle are making statements about the way in which they wish to live their lives. It is the expression of a desire for a change in human activity in favour of sustainable modes of behaviour. Of course, this a fine political aspiration, but the issue is whether, in domestic law, it can be given any legal effect.

UNRAVELLING THE PRECAUTIONARY PRINCIPLE

Time does not allow a long consideration of the development of the precautionary principle and, in any case, there is no shortage of such analyses.[12] I simply wish to take, as a working definition of the precautionary

---

9   House of Commons, *The BSE Inquiry: The Report*, Phillips Report, 2000, London: House of Commons (www.bseinquiry.gov.uk).

10 See *op cit*, Beck, fn 2, p 161, n 1.

11 Eg, Ramm, HH, 'The precautionary principle: a phony political-scientific paradigm' (1999) 111 The New Australian 15; Hathcock, JN, *Assuring Science-Based Decisions – No Need for a Separate Precautionary Principle in Risk Analysis for Foods*, 1999, Washington DC: Council for Responsible Nutrition.

12 See, eg, O'Riordan, T and Cameron, J, 'The history and contemporary significance of the precautionary principle', in O'Riordan, T and Cameron, J, *Interpreting the Precautionary Principle*, 1994, London: Earthscan; McIntyre, O and Mosedale, T, 'The precautionary principle as a norm in customary environmental law' (1997) 9 Journal of Environmental Law 221; Freestone, D, 'The road from Rio: international environmental law after the Earth Summit' (1994) 6 Journal of Environmental Law 193; Freestone, D, [contd]

principle, Art 15 of the UNCED Rio Declaration of 1992. It is worth noting in passing the lack of precise definition in European Union (EU) Law, which might otherwise have provided a starting point, notwithstanding the incorporation of the principle into Art 174 of the European Community Treaty. Article 15 states that:

> ... where there are threats of serious or irreversible damage, lack of full scientific certainty shall not be used as a reason for postponing cost-effective measures to prevent environmental degradation.

It is worth considering this principle carefully and in the light of the EU Communication, which addresses other Community Institutions and the Member States on the manner in which the Commission will seek to arrive at decisions on risk containment.[13]

Perhaps the first issue of note on reading Art 15, is the application of the principle to serious or irreversible damage to the environment. Presumably, outside this framework, there is no requirement for the application of the principle, an important limitation in view of the criticism that the precautionary principle may represent 'a deeply conservative Luddite reaction to social advances and ecological change'.[14] The Communication on the Precautionary Principle shows an awareness of this, and points to the need to remember the impossibility of removing all risks of an activity.

Moreover, there must exist a threat of such damage. Here, we hit a problem caused by our loose vocabulary of risk. Earlier risk was described as uncertainty, but this itself comes in different forms. My chances of surviving my train journeys to London next week are uncertain as tragic experience shows, but no doubt actuarial figures could be presented to offer a probabilistic analysis of my chances. However, there are many other forms of uncertainty about which I may worry and for which such analysis is not available because the probability is unknown. Yet, for me to worry about such risk, I must have some indication that an untoward event is possible even if its probability is unknown.

It follows, therefore, that the precautionary principle occupies a certain territory in which a threat is recognised but beset by uncertainty. This may be because some element of the risk equation remains unknown. To take an earlier example, we know of new variant CJD, but not of its prevalence, and

---

12 [contd] 'The precautionary principle', in Churchill, R and Freestone, D, *International Law and Global Climate Change*, 1991, London: Graham and Trotman; Backes, CW and Verschuuren, JM, 'The precautionary principle in international, European and Dutch wildlife law' (1997) 9 Colorado Journal of International Law and Policy 43.

13 European Commission, *Communication on the Precautionary Principle*, 2 February 2000 – COM (2000) 1 final.

14 See Holder, J, 'Safe science? The precautionary principle in UK environmental law', in Holder, J, *The Impact of EC Environmental Law in the United Kingdom*, 1997, London: John Wiley, for a critique of this view.

without that information we cannot calculate the true probability of harm. More problematic is this situation in which we can foresee the possibility of serious harm, but remain entirely unsure of its existence. One would not react in the same way faced with these different species of 'risk', since we would expect far greater caution in a situation in which a hazard (though not its prevalence) is known, than where a hazard can merely be anticipated. Having said that, if irreversible damage might result, then it is right to invoke caution. This approach is endorsed by the EU communication, which states that the precautionary principle presupposes that potentially dangerous effects of an activity have been identified, even though the precise impact cannot be determined with certainty.

Critics of this viewpoint assert that this involves action in the absence of scientific certainty. This assumes, however, that such certainty is achievable, and there are many reasons why this is not so. Science is a matter of interpretation, and scientific proof a point at which consensus is reached on a particular hypothesis. This is not absolute proof and is likely to be based on all manner of soft assumptions.[15] In real world contexts, these may not apply, denying the validity of the hypothesis. In any case, it is not generally the scientists that will be responsible for policy based upon their findings, so that assumptions, understood by the scientific community, may not be shared by policy makers.[16] One of the strengths of the precautionary principle is that it recognises a realm outside of the 'scientific' and begins to address risk perceptions. This point is considered further below.

The next striking point about the Art 15 formulation of the precautionary principle is that the threat of serious or irreversible damage does no more than create an agenda for the consideration of cost-effective measures to be taken. In other words, it will lead to some form of risk assessment, which itself may lead to a proportionate form of protective measure. This is a far cry from the model presented both by its critics and by certain interest groups that the application of the precautionary principle, in the face of scientific uncertainty, must lead to an absolute ban on proposed activity or development. A 1998 definition propounded by the Commission Directorate for Health and Consumer Protection suggested the following:

> The Precautionary Principle is an approach to risk management that is applied in circumstances of scientific uncertainty reflecting the need to take action in the face of a potentially serious risk without waiting for the results of scientific research.[17]

---

15 Wynne, B and Mayer, S, 'How science fails the environment' (1993) 138 New Scientist 33.

16 I have pursued some of these themes further in my paper in Lowry, J and Edmonds, R, *Environmental Protection and the Common Law*, 1999, Oxford: Hart.

17 Quoted in National Consumer Council, *Public Health and the Precautionary Principle*, 2000, London: NCC.

The Commission Communication emphasises that the principle sets up a 'structured decision making process' with the structure 'provided by the three elements of risk analysis', namely assessment, management and communication.[18]

There can be little doubt that some of this language is influenced by the EU reaction to the finding by the appellate body of the World Trade Organisation (WTO), in the EU/US beef hormones case, that:

> ... by maintaining sanitary measures which are not based on a risk assessment, (the EU) has acted inconsistently with the requirements of contained in Article 5.1 of the Sanitary and Phytosanitary Agreement.[19]

Having said that, this decision should not be read as suggesting that the precautionary principle does not include risk assessment. There is no doubt that the EU found itself in difficulty in the case, having sought to justify a permanent rather than a provisional ban, where the latter would have allowed explicit application of precaution. Proceeding for a permanent ban on imports of beef, when similar hormones are to be found in European pig meat, was always likely to prove difficult, especially because:

> The EU side simply had not produced any evidence that indicated that growth hormones were being used on a scale that allowed intakes to vary significantly from those to which people are naturally exposed.[20]

In rather more straightforward language:

> ... the EU never got past first base for it was found not to have carried out the necessary investigations ...[21]

Unfortunate though this decision was for the application of the precautionary principle, it may have done some good in leading to the Commission producing, if not a well defined enunciation of the principle, at least a rule based communication, which begins to give the principle some meaning as a legal instrument. Indeed, after the WTO decision, Leon Brittan stated before a WTO Symposium on Trade:

> I accept the legitimacy of the concept of precaution in the field of environment and health. However, there are dangers in allowing a general open-ended principle without defining what it means and in what circumstances it can be used.[22]

---

18 See *op cit*, European Commission, fn 13, p 8.
19 *WTO Appellate Body Report on EC Measures concerning Meat and Meat Products (Hormones)*, complaint by the USA WT/DS26/ABAB/R; AB – 1997 – 4 PH June 1999, Jan 1998.
20 Holmes, P, 'The WTO *Beef Hormones* case: a risky decision?' (2000) 10 Consumer Policy Review 61.
21 See *op cit*, National Consumer Council, fn 17, p 19.
22 Quoted in the newsletter, (2000) *European Access*, June, p 11.

The Communication is still thin on precise definition and leaves open some difficulties of thresholds that might govern the point at which the principle can be invoked. However, given the problems of the WTO Appellate Body in grappling with problems of 'sufficient scientific evidence' in the *Beef Hormones* case, the Commission may have taken the wisest path in laying down general guidelines to govern the application of the principle. These demand that action should be proportionate, non-discriminatory, consistent and subject to cost/benefit analysis and to periodic review. All of these guidelines can be informed the by wider jurisprudence of EU Law, allowing for the development of a working legal doctrine.[23] This is something to be further explored, but before doing so I wish to consider further the question of risk.

RISK PERCEPTIONS AND REGULATION

The beef hormones dispute led to suggestions that Europe was applying the precautionary principle but that the USA was not prepared to do so, and that the invocation of the principle by the EU was naked trade protectionism.[24] However, as Groth points out, there are examples of the USA acting in the face of European food scares to ban imports including British beef (post-BSE) and Belgian poultry (following dioxin contaminated feed).[25] The difference between the US and the European approach, as reflected in attitudes to GM crops, seems to be what might be encompassed within the process of risk assessment.[26] Stripped of any social imperative towards precaution in the face of uncertainty, the US approach is much more constrained towards a narrower stance of precaution only where science dictates. But, there is a problem here; effective risk assessment may have to grapple with uncertainty especially since, as has been argued, positions of 'certainty' may be socially determined. That also suggests that there should be room for other dimensions than the 'scientific'. Indeed, this categorisation is problematic, since the framing of the issue with which science is charged may be a product of political determination.

GM crops are a surprisingly good example of this, since the USA was prepared to proceed on a case by case basis with a technical evaluation of each genetically modified product at the expense of asking larger questions of the

---

23 Though there may be greater difficulty with the notion that responsibility for producing scientific evidence may be assigned amongst different parties.

24 See *op cit*, National Consumer Council, fn 17; and Groth, E, *Science, Precaution and Food Safety*, 2000, New York: Consumers Union of US (available at www.biotech-info.net).

25 *Ibid*, Groth, pp 7–8.

26 Jasonoff, S, 'Between risk and precaution – reassessing the future of GM crops' (2000) 3 Journal of Risk Research 277.

whole enterprise. Whatever the outcome, it is hard to deny the sense of exploring the wider dimensions of genetic modification on biodiversity and on a range of other environmental and social issues. This may cause us to reflect on the problems of producing, at a global level, overarching agreements such as those of the WTO, where the background values and cultural assumptions underlying scientific enquiry may vary greatly. But, if we are to engage in this task, then it may be important to learn from each other, and realise that the process may begin, not end, with a technical evaluation. From there, there will need to be a process addressing issues that lie beyond the narrow consideration of 'good science'. To put it another way, the precautionary principle should lead to risk assessment, but that assessment must pay regard to public perceptions of risk. Rather than seeking to separate out the 'scientific' from the 'political', it would make sense to allow that the scientific is often political and that decisions based on science are likely to have a political dimension.

LEGAL APPLICATION OF THE PRECAUTIONARY PRINCIPLE

In seeking to identify a role for the precautionary principle in the British courts, the woolly status of the principle in EU law is less than helpful. Mention in Art 174 achieves little of itself and Hession and Macrory conclude that that, while the principle may be of general application to Community legislative action, it is unlikely to be justiciable or directly applicable.[27] Indeed, it was this type of approach by the ECJ in Peralta that allowed the Court of Appeal, in the case of *R v Secretary of State for Trade and Industry ex p Dudderidge*,[28] to refuse to make a reference to the ECJ, and to uphold the decision of the Queen's Bench Division.[29] This was to the effect that the Secretary of State might wish to act in accordance with the precautionary principle, but there was certainly nothing in the EC Treaty that obliged him to do so. *Dudderidge* represents the most detailed review of the application of the principle in the English courts, but not the only one.

---

27 Hession, M and Macrory, R, 'Maastricht and the environmental policy of the Community: legal issues of a new environment policy', in O'Keeffe, D and Twomey, PM, *Legal Issues of the Maastricht Treaty*, 1994, London: Wiley, p 151.

28 (1996) 71 P & CR 350.

29 [1995] Env LR 151. The High Court demonstrated a clear scepticism about the scope of the Electricity Act 1989 powers available to the Secretary of State similar to the approach taken in *R v Greenwich LBC ex p Williams* (1995) unreported, 19 December – a case on road closures under the Road Traffic Regulation Act 1984; see Jarvis, F, 'Warning use precaution when proceeding' (1996) 9 Utilities Law Review 185.

In three cases in the year 2000, challenges to decisions on waste management licensing sought to invoke the application of the precautionary principle, only to meet judicial resistance in broadly similar forms. In *R v Environment Agency ex p Turnbull*,[30] Jowitt J considered an argument that the precautionary principle should apply to a decision to exempt from waste licensing the storage of meat and bonemeal following cattle slaughter in the aftermath of the BSE outbreak. In response, the judge stated that 'the precautionary principle is best understood as being something which illuminates the application of the (waste licensing) Regulations'. The application was dismissed. In *R v Leicestershire CC ex p Blackfordby and Booththorpe Action Group*,[31] an attempt was made to place some reliance on this thin line of *dicta* in order to argue that the precautionary principle ought at least to 'illuminate' the Waste Framework Directive and the Waste Licensing Regulations 1994. This was in the context of a decision to grant permission for waste disposal by landfill. The argument met with the rejoinder that the principle had no direct effect and, in so far as the planning authority had followed the requirements of the relevant legislation, any application of the precautionary principle had been met. This judicial line was employed in a later landfill case, *R v Derbyshire CC ex p Murray*.[32]

Similar tactics of what Jane Holder has described as 'evasion'[33] occurred in *Gateshead MBC v Secretary of State for the Environment*[34] in which an applicant argued that to grant planning permission for a clinical waste incinerator in the absence of knowledge as to how pollution controls might be used to protect human health was a denial of the precautionary principle. By asserting that the grant of planning permission would not restrict the adequate control of the site by the regulators, the courts deny the reality of the effect of the permission. By doing so, the courts place a heavy burden on the applicant of showing that the facility is so hazardous that no reasonable authority should allow it. This grim catalogue of cases is redressed only by the odd case[35] in which support for a decision of the administration has been bolstered by the case for precaution, but such cases offer little of lasting use in developing a workable principle.

---

30 [2000] Env LR 715.
31 [2001] Env LR 35.
32 [2001] Env LR 494.
33 See *op cit*, Holder, fn 14, n 13.
34 [1994] Env LR 37.
35 Eg, *Alfred McAlpine v Secretary of State for the Environment* [1994] NPC 138; and *Mid Kent Water v Secretary of State for the Environment* (1997) unreported, 26 March.

Elsewhere in the common law world, accommodating the precautionary principle has not proved so difficult. Most famously, in Australia, in *Leatch v National Parks and Wildlife Service*,[36] although the relevant statute (unusually for modern Australian environmental law) made no mention of the precautionary principle, it was said to be a 'keystone' of the court's approach to conservation:

> ... the precautionary principle is a statement of common sense ... its premise is that uncertainty or ignorance exists concerning the nature or scope of environmental harm (whether this follows from policies, decisions or activities) decision makers should be cautious.

The judge in that case has cited in a paper a number of other Australian decisions in which this line of argument has been developed.[37] He also points out that the precautionary principle has been said to apply in New Zealand, where, in *Greenpeace, New Zealand v Minister for Fisheries*,[38] it was said that, when facts underpinning a decision were in dispute, it was not necessary always to take the most conservative decision, but the relevant material had to be weighed with great care, and where 'uncertainty or ignorance exists, decision makers must be cautious'. Not, it should be added, that Greenpeace succeeded in overturning the decision of the Minister – in line with a number of cases referred to below.

However, from this promising beginning, the development of the precautionary principle in Australia has not been entirely happy.[39] This is notwithstanding its early incorporation into a wide range of legislation, often within the objects clause of the Act itself. It is not only the legislatures that have embraced international law in this respect, but the courts too have been willing, along the lines of *Leatch* above to accept the doctrine often as customary international law of domestic relevance.[40] Yet, it seems though the legislation has come in advance of any accepted process of how the principle

---

36 (1993) 81 LGERA 270.

37 Stein, P, 'Are decision makers too cautious with the precautionary principle?', paper from Land and Environment Court Annual Conference (www.agd.nsw.gov.au).

38 (1995) unreported, 27 November. In India, too, in *Vellore Citizens Welfare Forum v Union of India* 1995 (5) SCC 647, the precautionary principle was said to govern the law of India and to be implied not only in various environmental statutes, but in the constitution itself. In *AP Pollution Control Board v Nayudu* 1999 (1) UJ (SC) 426, it was said that: 'Precautionary duties must not only be triggered by the suspicion of concrete danger, but also by (justified) concern or risk potential.'

39 Fisher, E, 'Is the precautionary principle justiciable?' (2001) 13 Journal of Environmental Law 315.

40 Barton, C, 'The precautionary principle in Australia: its emergence in legislation and as a common law doctrine' (1998) 22 Harvard Environmental Law Review 509.

might be applied, and the judges left with this task have proved cautious and unready to respond to the challenge. In fact, the most common outcomes of the case law in Australia would seem to be either to invoke the principle as an endorsement of administrative decision making, rather than as a tool for challenge,[41] or to accept that the background environmental law already incorporated the precautionary principle.[42] We see similar strategies emerging in England and Wales.[43]

The lesson here would seem to be that, even if one goes beyond *Dudderidge* to accept that the principle is rather more than a policy instrument, so as to allow its application in matters of judicial review, little may be gained unless there exists some practical or procedural mechanism with which to measure the moves towards precaution. This is no easy task if one is to address the questions inherent in the precautionary principle: Is the potential damage serious or irreversible? What is the state of scientific knowledge in relation to this threat? Are there cost-effective solutions, including, presumably, abandoning the planned development because the environmental costs will outweigh any economic advantage? The difficulty here might be demonstrated by the experience of Pakistan. There, Lau has reported,[44] the assertion of constitutional rights in public interest litigation to oppose the siting of an electrical grid station in a residential neighbourhood of Islamabad. This led to the application of the precautionary principle in view of the potential breach of constitutional guarantees threatened by the development. The court refused to determine the issues itself but mandated wide ranging public consultation and expert evaluation overseen by a court appointed scientific commissioner.[45]

Such solutions seem a long way from the sphere of English administrative law. Oddly, private law may be more capable of this type of task. Notions of breach of duty in the law of tort have attempted commonly to balance the risk of harm against the practicability of precautions in the light of the importance attaching to the underlying objective being pursued.[46] However, to pursue this type of approach would demand so elaborate an enquiry on matters of scientific dispute that the utility of invoking the principle in the public interest might well be lost given the costs and complexities that would attach. In any

---

41 See, eg, *R v Resource Planning and Development Commission ex p Aquatas Property Ltd* (1998) 100 LGERA 1; *Bridgetown Greenbushes Friends of the Forest v Dept of Conservation and Management* (1997) WAR 102. And, perhaps most famously, *Friends of Hinchinbrook Society v Minister for the Environment* (1997) 142 ALR 632.

42 As in *Optus v City of Kensington and Norwood* [1998] SAEDRC 480.

43 See *op cit*, Holder, fn 14, n 13.

44 Lau, M, 'The right to public participation: public interest litigation and environmental law in Pakistan' (1995) 4 RECIEL 49.

45 *Zia v WAPDA* 1994 SC 6993.

46 See the judgment of Judge Learned Hand in *United States v Carroll Towing Co* (1947) 159 F (2d) 169, p 173.

case, it seems apparent that, even at the invitation of the Human Rights Act 1998, the courts are disinclined to engage in the review of the merits of administrative decisions.[47] As one Australian Judge stated, such an approach might lead to 'interminable forensic argument'.[48]

CONCLUSION: TOWARDS A (RE)SOLUTION

The trick must be to search for a model of review within which no attempt is made to best guess the regulatory determinations, but without leaving the courts powerless, and the precautionary principle a dead letter. Turning to the principle itself, it consists of a simple device of demanding regulatory caution in the face of a threat of serious environmental harm. Not only ought this to be possible for English administrative law, but the principles of review are now clearly laid down in the Commission's communication.[49] That communication clearly envisages the move towards the working of the precautionary principle at a formal, procedural level – otherwise why consider issues such as the reversal of burdens of proof? It would seem to be only a matter of time before the status of the principle, as a matter of EU law, is subject to detailed review by the European Court of Justice.

At such a point, the English courts may be forced to adopt some form of review that does more than pay mere lip service to the principle, on the basis that EU environmental legislation itself must constitute the last word on precautionary action. Quite what might be required is clear from the communication, which seeks a proportionate and consistent response to risk through a proper process of balancing environmental costs and benefits. While the courts would have little enthusiasm for making substantive determinations of what precaution demands, and second-guessing political or administrative decisions, court supervision of the process of decision making is a different matter. Indeed, the courts are already aware following the passage of the Human Rights Act 1998 that their widened jurisdiction might lead to changes in the nature of judicial review.

This remark might surprise those who see the initial run of cases in the planning arena has showing a most cautious approach of their new powers. However, the insistence by the House of Lords in *Alconbury* of any role of judicial review beyond the question of the legality of decision making comes

---

47 See *Alconbury* [2001] 2 WLR 1389; and *R v Secretary of State for the Home Office ex p Daly* [2001] 2 WLR 1622, discussed below.

48 *Per* Talbot J in *Nicholls v Director General of National Parks and Wildlife* (1994) 84 LGERA 397, p 419.

49 See *op cit*, European Commission, fn 13, n 12; and see Fisher, E, 'The European Commission's Communication on the precautionary principle' (2000) 12 Journal of Environmental Law 403.

at a price. The House of Lords were faced with the concession by the Secretary of State in that case that, by reason of the creation and application of policy matters, he could not be said to constitute an 'independent and impartial' tribunal for the purposes of Art 6 of the convention when determining the planning matters at issue in the case. But, in convention case law, this need not matter if the decision maker is subject to control of a judicial body with full jurisdiction.[50] In suggesting that such control did not have to consist of a rehearing of the merits of a decision, Lord Slynn found himself praying in aid Art 230 of the EC Treaty, by way of suggesting that, even within the European Court of Justice, review of executive action was limited to issues of legality. Lord Slynn was forced to concede, however, that the principle of proportionality applied, and he went on to state that:

> There is a difference between that principle and the approach of the English courts in *Associated Provincial Picture Houses Ltd v Wednesbury Corporation*.[51] But the difference in practice is not as great as sometimes supposed ... I consider that even without reference to the Human Rights Act the time has come to recognise this principle as part of English administrative law, not only when they are dealing with Community acts but also when they are dealing with acts subject to domestic law.

While it may take some stretch of the imagination to equate what was once described as the 'crude bludgeon of the *Wednesbury* principle'[52] with the doctrine of proportionality, Lord Slynn was picking up on what has become a powerful movement in recent administrative law. In *R v Ministry of Defence ex p Smith*,[53] Lord Bingham, the then Master of the Rolls, seemed to herald a new approach when he accepted the submission of David Pannick QC to the effect that: '... the more substantial the interference with human rights, the more the

---

50   *Albert and Le Compte v Belgium* (1983) 5 EHRR 533.

51   [1948] 1 KB 223.

52   *Per* Laws J in *R v Cambridgeshire HA ex p B* (1995) 23 BMLR 1.

53   [1996] QB 517, curiously, this case comes hard on the heels of the Master of the Rolls rejecting such heightened scrutiny in *R v Cambridge HA ex p B* [1995] 2 All ER 129, in which Laws J, at first instance ([1995] FLR 1055) suggested that what was at stake was a right to life.

court will require by way of justification before it is satisfied that the decision is reasonable ...' This *dicta* was seized on by Laws LJ in *R v Secretary of State for the Home Department ex p Mahmood*[54] and developed by Phillips MR in the same case into three significant principles. First, the role of the courts is supervisory so that, even in human rights cases the court will intervene only where the decision falls outside a range of reasonable responses. However, secondly, where a decision affected human rights, the court would subject the decision to 'anxious scrutiny'. Finally the court could require 'substantial justification' for an interference with human rights in order to be satisfied that the response falls within the reasonable range, and, again, the more substantial the interference, the greater the justification required.

The 'general tenor' of this approach has been endorsed by the House of Lords in *R v Secretary of State for the Home Department ex p Daly*,[55] in which Lord Steyn talks openly of the doctrine of proportionality. In so far as his Lordship departs from the approach, it is to go further while disavowing any role in reviewing merits. Thus, in modifying the range of reasonable responses test, he states that the doctrine of proportionality 'may require the reviewing court to assess the balance which the decision maker has struck'. In undertaking scrutiny of 'the relative weight accorded to interests and considerations', the proportionality test 'may go further' than traditional grounds of review. As Lord Steyn points out, in *ex p Smith*, the anxious scrutiny of the rights of the homosexual soldiers nonetheless produced a denial of Art 8 rights overturned by the ECHR. In his Lordship's view, the intensity of the review should be:

> ... guaranteed by the twin requirements that the limitation of the right was necessary in a democratic society, in the sense of meeting a pressing social need, and the question whether the interference was really proportionate to the legitimate aim being pursued.

---

54 [2001] 1 WLR 840 – for the development of proportionality principles, see also *R v Secretary of State for the Home Department ex p Launder* [1997] 1 WLR 839; *R v Lord Saville of Newdigate ex p A* [1999] 4 All ER 860; and the Privy Council decision in *De Freitas v Permanent Secretary of the Ministry of Agriculture Fisheries Lands and Housing* [1999] 1 AC 69.

55 *Per* Lord Steyn, p 1635.

This, of course, is part of human rights jurisprudence, but this makes the *dicta* of Lord Slynn in *Alconbury*, that the principle of proportionality is part of English administrative law in its own right, of some importance. Even if one is not so confident about the location of the principle in domestic law, it may be increasingly invoked as part of EU law as Lord Slynn allows. More than this, we see in *ex p Smith* a willingness to apply the principle where Treaty rights are at stake (in the form of the European Convention on Human Rights prior to the passage of the Human Rights Act 1998). There would seem to be little conceptual difficulty in adopting the anxious review, as espoused in *ex p Daly*, in situations what is at stake is not a threat to a human right but the threat of serious or irreversible damage to the environment.

This limited solution of second order scrutiny of decisions may disappoint those hoping for more from the precautionary principle. But, the alternative is to drag the courts into the task of risk assessment. Risk society is a society that requires more involvement and more democratic opportunity to control ecological risk. It is implicit that the old model of technical decision making by unaccountable expert determination cannot continue if we are to address the social and moral dimensions of such decisions, and if we are to redefine what we accept as 'progress'. Greater democratic input implies a greater transparency in public and private decisions that impact on the environment, and much greater opportunities for participation in decisions from which people have been excluded. A doctrine of proportionality by demanding an assessment of the relative weight of competing interests has the capacity, over time, to secure these values to the benefit of the environment.